I0458874

MORE THAN A CONQUEROR

A Toolkit for Young Thrivers

ORVIN T. KIMBROUGH

Stonebrook Publishing
St. Louis, Missouri

A STONEBROOK PUBLISHING BOOK
©2025 Orvin Kimbrough
This book was guided in development and edited
by Nancy L. Erickson, https://nancylerickson.com

Hardcover ISBN: 978-1-955711-47-0
Softcover ISBN: 978-1-955711-46-3
eBook ISBN: 978-1-955711-48-7

www.stonebrookpublishing.net

PRINTED IN THE UNITED STATES OF AMERICA

"Wow! What a powerful story. Orvin Kimbrough's *More Than a Conqueror* is a powerful reminder that humble beginnings don't define your destiny. His message of faith, perseverance, and purpose gives young people the courage to keep dreaming and trust God through every trial."

—Cuonzo LaMar Martin
Head Men's Basketball Coach, Missouri State University

"*More Than a Conqueror* gives young readers practical principles to not just survive but thrive—it offers real hope and tools that last forever."

—Bishop M. Fulton Jones, Sr.
Friendly Temple MB Church

"Orv's story in *More Than a Conqueror* shows what **is** possible. His resilience—and the caring community that surrounded him—inspire and compel us to act."

—Rich McClure
Co-Chair, The Ferguson Commission
Former CEO, United Van Lines and Mayflower Transit

"*More Than a Conqueror* is a vulnerable, honest, and powerfully raw account of a life's journey that'll inspire young people to open their minds and hearts to what's possible. It's a vivid reminder that no matter the path, amazing things can happen through faith and hard work."

"For I know the thoughts that I think toward you, saith the Lord, thoughts of peace, and not of evil, to give you an expected end."
—Jeremiah 29:11 (KJV)

—Nicole Randall
Mathematics Department Chair, John Burroughs School

"Orvin Kimbrough's life is a radiant testament to triumph over trials, proving that adversity should never break you but, instead, ignite faith and bold action. This book is an essential guide that inspires readers to stay rooted in optimism through every storm. It teaches young people to harness the power of manifestation and faith, transforming pain into purpose and greatness. Anchored in divine belief, it reveals the inner strength to conquer all and rise *more than victorious.*"

—Krishna Chaitanya Kurnala
President, Stellar IT Solutions

Dedication

For my brother, **Cornelius Kimbrough**,
whose living was cut short, but whose spirit still pushes me to rise.
Your light reminds me that potential is sacred,
and time isn't promised.
To the fatherless and motherless, to those without direction,
this book is for the survivors who have felt overlooked at every
stage of their journey. It shows the heights we can reach when we
commit to strength and allow ourselves to dream big.

CONTENTS

CHAPTER 1

WELCOME TO MY LIFE

E very story has a beginning, but not every beginning is easy. Some of us start in places we didn't choose—surrounded by challenges, questions, and people who may not always understand us. But where you begin doesn't decide where you'll end up.

That's what this book is really about. It's about how to take the hardest parts of your story and turn them into strength. It's about what it means to thrive—to rise above the odds, grow through pain, and keep believing when it would be easier to give up.

A **thriver** is someone who doesn't just survive what happens to them—they learn from it, build from it, and use it to move forward. Thrivers don't wait for life to be perfect; they find a way to make meaning out of what they've been given.

So many of us have struggles. I certainly had mine. And yet, I made it. When people hear my story, they often ask, "How did you make it? How did you do that?" The truth is, I didn't always know I could. There were years I didn't believe I'd have a real family, years I couldn't imagine happiness, and years when money was a constant worry. But today, I have more joy than I ever thought possible, more success than I imagined, and a family who loves me deeply. That didn't happen by accident. It happened by holding on to certain principles and practicing them over and over again, even when life was hard.

Those principles became my **Thriver's Toolkit**, and they are the same set of tools that helped me turn pain into power and setbacks into stepping stones. You'll find them listed right after this introduction. These are the ideas that shaped how I think, live, and lead.

Each chapter of this book tells part of my story and shows how one or more of these principles came to life. And at the end of every chapter, you'll find a section called "Tools You Can Use." These short lessons connect directly back to the Thriver's Toolkit, and they will help you practice the same principles that helped me grow.

By the time you finish, you'll have built your own **Thriver's Toolkit**, one that helps you:

- Turn hard times into opportunities to grow.
- Build strong relationships that lift you up.
- Discover your worth and your unique voice.
- Keep learning, adapting, and dreaming bigger.

Life will test you. But you have everything you need inside to overcome. This book isn't about being perfect. It's about becoming stronger, wiser, and more hopeful with every step. So, take a breath, open your heart, and begin this journey with me. Because thriving isn't something that happens to you, it's something you choose every single day.

THE THRIVERS TOOLKIT: PERSONAL GROWTH PRINCIPLES

1. **Turn tough times into chances to grow.**

When tough things happen, use them to help you grow. Turn each problem into a way to get stronger and bounce back better.

Daily Thought: Even when things get tough, I'll do more than people expect and turn problems into ways to grow.

2. **Forgive others and let go of old hurts to move on.**

When you forgive people who hurt you, you'll free yourself from anger and bitterness. This lets you focus on good things coming up.

Daily Thought: I'll let go of anger today by forgiving others, so I can focus on my future.

3. **Stay strong and focused, and don't give up when things go wrong.**

Your drive to succeed, even when things keep changing, will make you stronger. The secret to beating problems and reaching your goals is to go forward when stuff gets hard. Stick to your path, even when it feels impossible, and your hard work will pay off in the end.

Daily Thought: I'll stay focused and strong today and keep bouncing back from problems with determination.

4. **Build and lean on a strong support team.**

Having people around you matters. Connect with friends and groups that lift you up. Get strength from people who believe in you and have your back.

Daily Thought: Today, I'll get strength from my friends, mentors, and positive connections.

5. <u>**Figure out what you're good at and what you need to work on.**</u>

Think about what you've been through so you can understand and accept what makes you special. This will help you feel more confident and know where you're going.

<u>Daily Thought:</u> I'll find and accept my unique strengths today.

6. **Work hard and stay dedicated.**

When you work hard and juggle lots of stuff, it shows that not giving up is key to success.

<u>Daily Thought:</u> I'll let my hard work and determination drive what I achieve today.

7. **Accept change and see it as a way to grow.**

Get used to new places and experiences so you can grow and find new chances.

<u>Daily Thought:</u> I'll accept change today to unlock chances to grow.

8. **Find inner peace through prayer and mindfulness.**

Praying and being mindful will give you the clear thinking and calm you need to handle life's good and bad times with a steady heart. Prayer can comfort and strengthen you, and it can help you find inner peace and keep things in perspective.

<u>Daily Thought:</u> I'll build calmness and clear thinking through prayer and mindful moments today, and I'll seek inner peace to handle my problems calmly.

9. **Know and celebrate your worth by seeing yourself as God sees you.**

Know your real value comes from how God sees you, not what the world says. Set healthy limits about who gets to influence your life, so you can make choices that respect your worth and boost your confidence.

Daily Thought: I'll honor my worth today by setting healthy limits and seeing myself as God sees me.

10. Face and overcome your fears.

Face your fears, like the fear of public speaking and tough topics, to show your courage and open up new chances. When you speak positive words about life, victory, and growth, you'll be able to handle and beat these fears.

Daily Thought: I'll open myself up to new chances today when I face my fears and speak positive words about life, victory, and growth.

11. Find and value mentors.

When you learn from mentors and sponsors, you'll get wisdom and help that will be key to how you grow as a person.

Daily Thought: I'll get wisdom and help from my mentors today.

12. Make your education a priority and embrace lifelong learning.

You need to value education and always hunt for new knowledge. This opens doors to fresh chances and gives you important skills for your path. When you learn throughout your life and gain new knowledge and skills, you'll stay ready for future challenges.

Daily Thought: I'll be prepared for the future because I value education and I learn constantly.

13. Keep a positive attitude, even when times get tough.

When you stay positive and hopeful, especially during hard times, you'll inspire the people around you and build up your own strength.

Daily Thought: I'll build strength in myself and others today by staying positive.

14. Set clear goals and plan for the future.

Clear goals that you create and chase will keep you focused and motivated. They'll turn your dreams into things you can actually achieve.

Daily Thought: Clear goals will help me turn my dreams into reality today.

15. Be grateful every day.

When you say thanks for the small and big things in life, you'll feel more joy and happiness, which makes your overall well-being better.

Daily Thought: I can improve my life today when I practice gratitude.

16. Give back to the community.

When you volunteer and help others, you make your life richer and create a positive impact on your community.

Daily Thought: I'll make a positive impact today by giving back to my community.

17. Develop strong leadership skills.

When you lead by example, communicate well, and inspire others, you build the key parts of your leadership path. You can boost your emotional intelligence and better motivate and guide people around you when you know yourself and control your reactions.

Daily Thought: I can inspire and guide others today when I know myself and control my reactions, which will strengthen my leadership through emotional intelligence.

18. Invest in healthy relationships.

When you invest in healthy relationships, you get support, love, and encouragement, and you make your journey more meaningful and fulfilling.

Daily Thought: I'll find support and fulfillment today when I build up healthy relationships.

19. Believe your future is positive.

When you believe in a positive future, even when things get tough, you can focus on your goals and inspire others to do the same.

Daily Thought: I'll stay focused on my goals today and believe in a positive future.

20. Be vulnerable enough to build real connections.

When you're open and honest about your struggles, you'll create deeper connections with others and find strength in being real.

Daily Thought: I can build real connections today by being vulnerable.

21. Have faith in yourself and your journey.

Faith in your abilities and trust in the process will give you confidence to face challenges and move forward with strong belief.

Daily Thought: I'll trust my abilities and the process today to handle challenges with confidence.

22. Celebrate both your wins and your losses.

When you recognize and celebrate all parts of your journey, including your wins and failures, you'll appreciate your progress and learn from what you've been through.

Daily Thought: I've come so far, no matter where I am right now, and I need to appreciate my journey.

23. **Step out in faith to overcome obstacles.**

Faith in a higher power or in your own potential can give you the strength and courage you need to beat life's obstacles. Let your faith guide you through tough times.

<u>Daily Thought:</u> I'll step out in faith today and trust that I have the strength to overcome any obstacle.

These success principles are the strategies I used on my journey. They show how I made it through challenges and reached my goals. As you start this book, I hope these ideas connect with you and inspire you to face your own journey with strength, hope, and determination. Remember, no matter where you start, you have the power to shape your future and make a difference in your life and the lives of others.

Please visit orvinkimbrough.com to sign up for our newsletter, to keep in touch, or to ask questions. Thank you for purchasing this book and writing a public review!

DISCLAIMER

This book is based on my life and experiences as I remember them. It isn't meant to criticize or harm anyone, living or deceased. Some names and details have been changed out of respect for privacy or because I no longer remember them exactly as they were.

While I've done my best to tell these stories truthfully, memory isn't perfect, and others may recall events differently. Some parts of this book touch on difficult experiences—including moments of pain, loss, and abuse—because they're part of my journey.

The thoughts and opinions shared here are my own and do not represent any organizations or individuals mentioned. This book is meant for reflection and encouragement, not as legal, medical, or professional advice. If you or someone you know is dealing with similar challenges, I encourage you to reach out to a trusted adult, counselor, or professional for support.

CHAPTER 2

HARD BEGINNINGS

"Obstacles don't have to stop you.
If you run into a wall, don't turn around and give up.
Figure out how to climb it, go through it, or work around it."
—Michael Jordan

"You only get one shot, do not miss your chance to blow."
—Eminem, "Lose Yourself"

was born into poor neighborhoods where, for generations, families didn't have much money. I was born into a home with sexual and physical abuse. I was born into schools that didn't have enough money and didn't help most people get better jobs or make more money. I wasn't just born into these things, I was raised in them. I lived in them for years. I experienced trauma and stress from living in dangerous areas with a lot of crime and because I grew up in foster care. Foster care was meant to help me heal from my trauma. No one thought it would help me become the leader of the second-biggest private bank in my town. I'm all these things, and this is my story.

When you don't come from much and can't get much, you learn to be scrappy. Everything becomes a tool for you to use. I was a scrappy kid. I used what I had to get what I wanted. I had anger problems, so I had to learn how to use that anger in good ways. I had trust problems, so I had to figure out which people I could trust to help me do things I couldn't do alone. The dictionary says scrappy means "having a tough and determined spirit."

Being scrappy also means never taking no for an answer. Scrappy means getting back up when someone knocks you down. It's staying mentally tough and being creative to find solutions. Scrappy is a "keep fighting" attitude.

Being scrappy means you know that setbacks will happen, but you won't let yourself fail completely. I didn't have many choices as a kid. If I was going to survive, it would be up to me.

It was a cold Saturday night on December 17, 2006, just days before my 31st birthday. I sat back in my recliner to watch *60 Minutes*. That Sunday, one of the segments was called "Lost and Found." The reporter set up the story about foster kids with these words:

> "They've been called some of the loneliest people on earth: children who were taken away from their parents due to neglect or abuse but were never adopted by new families. Stranded in the child welfare system, they move from foster homes to group homes. There are tens of thousands of these children. They have no one—not a single relative to visit on Christmas or their birthday."

That sounded just like me, and this seemed eerily close to my own story.

You won't find the hospital where I was born anymore. It was called Christian Welfare Hospital in East St. Louis, Illinois. Like many things that once stood in that community, it's gone now, erased by time. When it opened, it was one of only two hospitals in the city. But even then, not every part of the hospital worked the way it should. For a long time, there wasn't even a place for babies to be born safely. That's important to know, because it shows how some communities don't always have the same resources as others—not even the basics, like a safe hospital for new mothers and babies.

As years went by, East St. Louis changed a lot. New highways were built, and public housing projects moved in. These decisions might have looked good on paper, but they made life harder for many people already struggling. Poor families were pushed into neighborhoods that were already poor, and businesses began to leave. A few old buildings still stand as reminders of what used to be, but many others, including the hospital where I was born, are long gone.

That's where my story begins: in a city that was fighting to survive. A place known for its violence, its poverty, and its pain but also for its toughness, its pride, and its heart. After my father left, my mother moved us across the river to North St. Louis. It was another poor, mostly Black community, but it had deep roots and people who cared about each other.

That's where I learned how to survive *and* how to dream. I learned to use my imagination when there wasn't much to go around. I learned that sometimes taking a risk was the only way forward. And I learned about loss, the kind that shapes who you are before you even realize it.

But I'll always remember where I came from: a hospital that no longer exists, in a city that never stopped trying. A place where even the street signs were missing but where I began to find my way.

When my mom moved my two brothers, sister, and me to North St. Louis City, we followed the steps of those who'd fled the race riots in East St. Louis across the Mighty Mississippi. Our situation was tough. We were extremely poor, and though I don't remember my mom working much, she did what she could to provide for us.

The only thing I brought with me from East St. Louis was a powerful imagination. For young people, imagination is really important. Your imagination is important! It makes it possible to change things that seem impossible, turns chaos into calm, and lets you go places you might not experience otherwise.

I was in a place where people didn't have much money, a place where poverty and crime were everywhere, but because of my imagination, I sometimes felt like I could do anything, even fly like Superman. In fact, I started to think that maybe I was Superman. It was a fantasy I created because I didn't feel loved by my mom, I missed my dad, and I hated our poverty, our tiny one-bedroom apartment, our drug-filled North St. Louis neighborhood, and our constant hunger. I needed my imagination to protect me from all the bad things in life.

We had no food on many days, but not even hunger got in Superman's way. He was a bigger-than-life figure who had amazing powers that most children and adults were naturally drawn to. He could easily move a planet. He could travel faster than light. He had unlimited energy. No food, no water, no rest—no problem! But having no food was often my reality, and it was a big problem. I loved the fact that Superman couldn't be hurt by anything—except, of course, Kryptonite.

To me, poverty—especially when families had been poor for generations—was Kryptonite. It took away the natural power from people who were born with promise and potential. Because we were poor, I was limited in what I could do. It weakened my power and had been forced on me because I was unlucky enough to be born to a drug-addicted mom and an absent dad.

In 2013, a group of researchers studied how poverty affected St. Louis's Black community. The study proved what Black St. Louisans had known from experience for generations: living in North City was bad for your health, both physically and mentally.

It felt like a death sentence when I was growing up in North St. Louis, and it wasn't my imagination. I wasn't playing the victim. It was a harsh reality and an obstacle that I promised to overcome for my family, my community, and myself. It was like there was a system that had covered up the potential to have good health, money, education, and helpful politics, which all worked against me. Even after getting over these barriers, they're still present today. The system's influence continues, and it quietly reminds me of the hurdles I've overcome.

My story shows the power of the human spirit. If I did it—whatever *it* is—you can do it, too. Facing impossible odds can actually create greatness and beauty. Being an underdog can change you in deep and far-reaching ways, and it can open doors to opportunities, teach you wisdom, and show you paths that once seemed impossible.

This story isn't just my story. It's proof of the power of never giving up. It shows that it's important to choose a different path and understand that your stories and leadership are tied to your past and the community you care about. It's about knowing that, against all odds, achieving the unthinkable is something you can reach.

I did it, and you can too.

There were four kids in our family. My brother Antwon, who we called Mony, was eighteen months older than me. My younger brother, Cornelius, who we called NeNe, was eighteen months younger than me, and our sister, Carmen, who we called Niecy, was a couple years younger than NeNe. When we were really young, we were close, and Mony acted like our protector.

One time, someone broke into our apartment. Mom owed someone money and had been talking around the neighborhood about a check she'd gotten. Even though we'd put furniture in front of the door keep it closed, the man forced his way through our cheap wooden door, and Mony, who was eight or nine at the time, got between the man and our tiny apartment and screamed, "I'm going to mess you up!" The man slapped him, pushed past his skinny body, and got the check. After we picked ourselves up off the floor, we knew Mom was going to be pissed off, but Mom was always pissed off.

My little brother was about five, and my sister was barely out of diapers at three. She was like a baby doll, totally unable to care for herself. The four of us typically did everything together. Where one kid went, you usually saw the others. Our mother was gone a lot, so if we were ever allowed to go outside, it was only out front or in the alley. Mom was strict about us staying close to the apartment, so our view of outside was through a four-by-four window. We lived on the second floor, and if we stuck our bodies out far enough over the ledge, we could see for what seemed like miles.

Our apartment complex was considered neglected housing, and our landlord was a classic example of a slumlord. The apartments had lots of problems: peeling lead paint, rusty water faucets, tons of rats and roaches, and electrical and plumbing systems that didn't work right. There were always lots of women and children in the apartments where we lived and in the single-family homes nearby.

During summer and on weekends, we'd have rock fights with kids from the other buildings, and we threw stones at each other. I remember getting hit by a rock on my foot while running between the floors during one of these battles. The bottom of my left foot split open, and I bled really badly.

We also met in the alley to fight kids from the other building. We all wanted to prove that we weren't weak. Saying "Yo mama" was enough to make people angry in my neighborhood and schools. When I think about it today, it's stupid and silly, but back then, it made complete sense to fight someone who simply said, "Yo mama." We circled each other and sized each other up, pointing fingers and yelling insults at the other person. If we really wanted to make them mad, we'd push the other person's head as hard as we could with one finger before throwing punches.

When we weren't fighting, we played games we probably shouldn't have been playing—games we learned from watching adults, not realizing they weren't meant for kids. We were curious, and we copied what we saw, even when we didn't fully understand it. In a lot of ways, we were trying to make sense of a world that didn't make much sense to us.

My mom was addicted to drugs and alcohol. I remember going to the second floor and pushing the privacy rag out of the hole where the lock used to be. Mom was with several addicts, two men and one other woman, and she had a rope tied around her arm with a needle in it. She was barely awake. I was scared, but I stood as still as I could so I wouldn't be seen or heard.

I later learned that Mom had a problem with drugs called uppers and downers. Uppers make your mind and body feel stimulated, and they give you a temporary boost in being alert, having energy, and feeling good. But when it wears off, the person is exhausted and depressed. Mom's uppers included meth and cocaine. Downers were the opposite of uppers, and they slowed things down. Drugs like heroin, morphine, fentanyl are downers. They make you feel pleasure and relaxation like uppers do, but they've similar bad side effects. People who use opiates for a long time stop caring about anything and become depressed, and that's what happened to Mom.

Because she stayed up late, we did too. There were only three rooms in our apartment: the front room, a kitchen area, and a sleeping space. Mom slept in the front room next to the kitchen. I don't remember having any doors. Curtains prevented us from peering into the front room, but we could hear everything. Mom called this apartment a "shotgun apartment." When I asked why, she said it was because you could fire a shotgun from one end, and the shot would travel straight through and out the window onto the streets.

"It's a straight shot," she said.

My mother and the people she hung around with didn't go to work. I never saw them do anything useful. Without good examples, I started stealing things whenever I got the chance, just like everyone else I knew.

We slept in and got up late most days, whether school was in session or not. I missed a lot of school. I stayed home with my brothers and sister and listened to the women in our apartment complex talk about their soap operas. We could tell what time it was by what soap opera or TV show was on. Over the years, I started to like the shows too. But I spent most of my days watching my younger brother and sister and trying to find something to eat.

Always Hungry

I worried a lot that we wouldn't get enough food to eat, and we often didn't. We tried to make do with what we had. The government feeding program sometimes gave us bread, canned braunschweiger meat, cheese, powdered milk, and powdered eggs. That was good eating. When those items ran out, we ate sugar sandwiches if we had bread and sugar. Bread with mustard, mayonnaise, or just about any spread would satisfy our hunger for a little while.

My brother got good at making fried cornmeal mush. He mixed cornmeal with water, then deep fried it. Mom would disappear for hours and days at a time and leave us to take care of ourselves. I never understood why she was so angry when she came back and found out we'd been cooking. Once, we heard Mom coming up the steps. My brother had just fried up his cornmeal mush, and he rushed over to the window and threw out the food. I was so hungry I could've followed that food out the two-story window.

Mom came in and shouted, "What are you doing?"

"Nothing," we said together.

"You're doing something. I can smell it," she said. I never got the courage to ask Mom why she was so mad.

It couldn't have been because we were little kids cooking with an electric skillet, since sometimes we turned on the oven to heat the apartment. We usually ate the best for about a week at the beginning of every month when the welfare checks came. The food stamps or government food never lasted as long as we hoped. We got used to the hunger, but we never liked it.

I had a wild imagination as a kid. I loved Superman and CHIPs, a TV crime drama. I pretended I was a cop and was strong like Erik Estrada, "Ponch," as he was called, and I had the powers of Superman. Superman didn't have to worry about food. As a young boy on one of the days I didn't go to school, I broke into my neighbor's apartment to steal food. I wondered what Ponch or Superman would have thought about that decision, but I was desperate. For every choice, there's a consequence.

But I was living a hard life and wasn't worried about the consequences. To survive, I did desperate things, like waiting for the school cafeteria workers to throw away expired food. To me, food never expired. My oldest brother and I often scavenged through the dumpster to find food. Sometimes, the items were nicely bundled.

"Look," I would say, "all of that food is in the milkcrate!"

I've often wondered if that was just good luck or if the cafeteria ladies knew we'd be looking for food. I often begged the lunch lady for two meals and begged my classmates for their free breakfast and lunch tickets before and after school. They looked at me like I was pitiful, but I didn't care. I was hungry.

Sometimes, we'd get lucky in the alley behind our apartment.

"Look, Mony," I said in amazement. "There's some fried chicken that's only been half eaten. And look at these clothes!"

The clothes included underwear, jeans, and shirts and were about our sizes.

"We only need to swat away the bees and flies and separate the food that has maggots on it," I said.

We had what turned out to be a great meal. And the clothes also seemed perfectly fine to wear.

School

I wasn't particularly interested in school. The only reason I went to school was to eat and feel safe. When I went to school, I liked to get there early to be sure I ate breakfast.

However, I was very competitive with certain aspects of school. For example, I found great joy in memorizing my times tables. We would sometimes have competitions to see who could go from 1x1 to 12x12, and I loved the energy this created. Even though I didn't practice enough to ever be that good at it, I still liked it.

My favorite subjects were recess, lunch, and the end of school. I loved playing kickball during recess. I was pretty good at kicking the big red ball far and throwing the ball hard enough to tag out other kids. I usually aimed for their heads if the teachers weren't looking. We also played dodgeball; I loved being the last man standing. During lunch, I made it a point to try to eat as much as I could because I wasn't sure when I would get to eat again.

I hated sitting in class. My mind was typically on the stuff that wasn't being taught. Throughout grade school and somewhat into high school, I was labeled "special," mostly because I had difficulty learning, probably because I barely attended school, and when I did, I was hungry. When I did go to school, I craved attention, so I was disruptive in class, picked fights, and was always running hot. I never backed down from a fight.

Once, I spit gum in a White girl's fine hair to see what would happen. I knew if someone spit gum in my hair, I'd whip their tail, so it never happened to me. But if it had, the gum would just hit my tightly wound curls and drop to the floor. But she has stringy hair, and I wondered what would happen. She sat right in front of me, so the gum didn't have to go far from my juicy lips. I made sure the gum was nice and wet before I drew a deep breath and blew out like I was blowing out stubborn birthday candles.

The gum landed in her hair, and she screamed, "Why did you do that?" and looked back at me with a scowl.

All eyes were now on me. I slouched in my seat and said, "Do what?" trying to deflect attention.

The more she tried to untangle the gum, the more "oohs" I heard from the class. I saw trouble coming my way. I was sent to the principal's office and got suspended. I hadn't had a reason to spit gum at her other than the attention I got from being a nuisance. I guess I was just special. Being special meant that I had to go to some smaller classes and spent more time talking to counselors, designated mentors, therapists, and the principal.

I was also fascinated with learning to write in cursive. Cursive writing was like a foreign language. We had white tracing cardboard that we could take home to perfect our cursive writing. Because I was left-handed, I was always frustrated because my writing always smeared across the page, as if I'd wiped mud on the page. The lead pencil also left a black stain on the side of my hand.

Eh, I thought as I spit on my hand and wiped back and forth on my pants to clean it, *I should have been right-handed.* Our desks were for right-handed kids only, and I had to twist my body to write.

I would have been right-handed, but when I was a baby, I was crawling behind my older brother, and he didn't see me when he went into the bathroom. He pushed the door shut, which was three times his size. My mom said that I screamed so loud that she "about had a heart attack."

They couldn't save my right pinky finger. After that, Mom started putting things in my left hand so it would be my dominant hand.

Kids teased me all through childhood, saying, "You crippled" and calling me "four finger boy" and "nine and a half." I would lash right back at them. With each taunt, I grew angrier and angrier. So, I would fight and get suspended.

It seems like I was always out of school, but I didn't care because I could escape by watching the soap operas with the powerful Victor Newman of *The Young and the Restless*, who never let anyone push him around. While Victor stood his ground on TV, I felt a sense of strength and solace from my own battles.

Mom

My mother was a tall, busty, big-boned woman. She had caramel-colored skin and, from what I can recall, big brownish hair. She seemed to struggle with her value and worth, as shown by the string of men in her life, the drug-induced comas, and the fact that she often disappeared for hours, if not days, on end when she left us kids alone and unprotected.

Her name was Carolyn. She was an only child with no significant family connections. I have vague memories of visiting cousins, but it wasn't often. There were several men in and out of Mom's life, and she invited them into our lives by telling us they were our "uncles." Our uncles occasionally brought us food, and most of them smelled like a fast-food restaurant, like they'd doused themselves with fryer oil.

The one who seemed to go away and come back more than any of them was called Ulysses. We called him US. I think US was the father of my oldest brother, and he was no more than five feet tall. And he had an explosive temper. Mom and US argued and fought a lot, usually about, "Who are you doing?" Many times, they traded punches in jealous outbursts. They also lashed out at others who came in between their unstable relationship.

On one occasion, US returned home after a stint in jail and beat one of mom's boyfriends with a baseball bat, then dragged him down the back stairs of our apartment complex. Apparently, this boyfriend had slapped or pushed my oldest brother. The ambulance was called to cart him away, and US was once more on the run from the police. He ended up going to prison for a very long time after he robbed the local grocery store.

Sexual Abuse

When I was five, my mom started bringing a man named Curtis Jr. to the house. He was a stranger to me, but my mom said he was my uncle—Uncle Curtis. Uncle Curtis would show up sometimes and hang out with Mom and his brother, who was the father of my two younger siblings. Mom, Uncle Curtis, and his brother would sometimes drink and have what seemed like a good time together. One summer, he started coming around more often because "we were a handful," as Mom would say. Sometimes he slept in the area where us kids slept. There was always a lot of hugging and lap sitting.

"Come here," he would say, pointing in my direction.

Mom didn't have to tell us to be polite. "I'll whoop they tail if they don't mind me," she often said. I didn't want my tail whooped, so I "mined" adults. That meant "do what you're told."

I was often alone with Uncle Curtis, and I hated it when he came over. He started crossing lines that made me feel confused, scared, and trapped. He did things no adult should ever do to a child. I didn't have the words for it then, but what he did was wrong. It was abuse.

I felt frozen inside, like my body was there but my mind had to go somewhere else just to get through it. I was only five years old, and I didn't know how to stop it or who I could tell. When it was over, I'd sit quietly in a corner, trying to disappear. I was afraid every day, whether he was around or not.

His behavior got worse over time. One day when Uncle Curtis was at the house, Mom said she was going to take my younger

22

siblings to the park and leave me at home with him. I remember shaking, terrified of being alone with him.

I grabbed my mom's leg and begged, "Momma, don't leave me."

She pulled me off her leg and asked, "Boy, what's wrong with you?"

I didn't have the words to tell her what was wrong, and because Uncle Curtis was right there, I didn't want to say it out loud. Uncle Curtis always swore that if I ever told anyone what he was doing to me, "I will kill you, your brothers, and your sister." I believed him.

I finally found the words—shaky and small—to tell Mom that Uncle Curtis had been hurting me in ways that made me feel trapped and ashamed. I didn't know how to describe it, only that I needed it to stop. She said, "What do you mean? What is he doing exactly?" Enough tears streamed from my eyes to put out a fire. Feeling almost paralyzed from fear, I told her what Uncle Curtis had been doing to me. I knew he was going to kill me, but I didn't care. I would rather be dead than be left alone with him.

Mom stood still for what seemed like forever. She then went into her room and came back out with a shotgun and shouted at him, "I am going to kill you—do you hear me?"

I wanted her to kill him. But Curtis Jr.'s brother talked her out of killing him, and she called the police instead.

When they arrived and heard the story, I remember an officer asked, "Why didn't you shoot him?" when they arrested Curtis.

Mom told me, "Baby, you're going to have to testify in court." I didn't know what the words *testify* or *court* meant, but over time, I remember talking to several White people and becoming even more afraid.

I showed up at the courthouse, and a kind White lady said, "Once you tell the truth about what happened to you, we're going to give you some money."

That made me happy and gave me the energy to go through with it. I was always hungry, and we needed the money.

That was when I learned the words *molestation* and *rape*. I told as much about what he'd done to me as I could and answered a lot of questions. I remember getting some money in a small manila envelope. Later, Mom said that Curtis Jr. would be in jail for a long time and that I would be safe.

After that, everything changed for me. I'd been a victim of and had seen sexual abuse and sexual assault, which was a trauma that could have slowed or stopped my development. Certain smells triggered those awful memories. I couldn't escape my thoughts, whether I was asleep or awake. I couldn't get over the pain. Despite my mother's assurance that "you will be safe," safety seemed far off to me.

Losing Mom

My mother once told me, "You're a mistake, and I don't love you."

Those were harsh words, but I felt like it was the alcohol and drugs speaking and not my mother. But still, it made me feel like I was naked and anyone could see and do anything to me, that there was no one to care for me. *Maybe I am a mistake,* I thought. Not having anyone to care for me made me hard. Not having anyone to care for me made me bitter. I got mad easily and always wanted to fight, but my relationship with my mother never got better.

One morning, I woke up early—and very hungry. I got up from the floor where I slept and went to the kitchen to see what I could eat. There was only a box of saltine crackers in the refrigerator. We kept food that normally belonged in the pantry in the refrigerator because of the roaches and mice. When we turned on the lights, the roaches would scatter, but the mice didn't budge when we opened the bin at the bottom of the fridge where we kept potatoes when we had them. They were always there falling over themselves. It was disgusting.

Because of my mom's addictions, any aid we got from the state went straight into her veins. She was a chronic drug user. She'd use when she woke up, and she fell asleep using, a rubber wire tied around her left arm while her right hand injected the drugs. So, I wasn't surprised when I left the kitchen and found her sleeping in the living room. I wanted to ask her if I could eat some crackers. We had to ask to eat because food was so hard to come by. When she didn't answer, I started shaking her.

"Momma, Momma, wake up!"

She still didn't wake up. I continued to shake her, and again, there was no response. By this time, my two brothers and sister were up. We knew something was wrong. My mom's face looked blue. Because we didn't have a phone, I hurried to the back of our shotgun apartment, kicked up the board that was wedged against the door to keep it locked (because we had no lock), and rushed across to a neighbor's apartment. I was banging violently on her door.

I screamed, "Something's wrong with Momma!"

"Huh?" she said.

I yelled once more, "Something is wrong! She's not moving!"

The neighbor called 911 and told them we needed help and where we lived. Despite all the noise and commotion, Mom didn't move.

Finally, the paramedics arrived. "What happened?" they yelled.

"We don't know," I said. "She normally wakes up. Her face is a different color than usual," I said.

The paramedics tried to bring my mom back to life, but they couldn't. We huddled together near her still body and watched nervously when they pronounced her dead. She was only twenty-eight years old.

We were sad for Mom. And we were sad for ourselves. We weren't sure where we were going to live or if we would ever live together again. We didn't understand that death was final, and we didn't know of any family except the four of us. The police asked a lot of questions about our "next of kin." We didn't have any relatives that we knew of.

Before the police came, we'd concocted a scheme to say that our next-door neighbor was our aunt. I don't remember why, but that lie fell apart quickly. Then, a light bulb turned on! We remembered a cousin who lived on the next street over. Mom had taken us there a couple of times.

We hopped into the police cruiser, and in a matter of minutes, we pulled up in front of a large yellow and green home. On that day, we became parentless wards of the state. Frozen in grief, I often found myself staring into space and thinking about my mom, not wanting to believe she was gone for good. It was overwhelming.

Over the next few days, my emotions were in chaos and were firing in all directions. I was happy that I might be able to eat when I was hungry, but I was mostly sad, angry, and disappointed. I was depressed and filled with anxiety. I was so angry and disappointed in Mom—for killing herself with drugs, for what she'd allowed Uncle Curtis to do to me, for not fighting harder to overcome what I now know as oppressive poverty, and for my hunger.

I was just about to start third grade when Mom died, and a few weeks after that, I found out that I had to repeat the second grade. I was so embarrassed. Not only had I lost Mom, but I lost all my friends because I was a special stupid kid.

After Mom's death and being held back that year, I knew that not every relationship lasts for life, including those with family and friends. It also taught me that some of the things I get in life are things I deserved—like being held back—and some things I didn't deserve, like Mom dying without ever telling me that she actually did love me.

Tools You Can Use:

Life doesn't always start out being fair, and sometimes it feels like you're carrying more than your share. But tough beginnings can shape strong minds and stronger hearts.

1. **Use what you have.** You may not have everything you want, but you probably have enough to take the next step. Resourcefulness is a true kind of strength.
2. **Keep showing up.** Even when life feels unfair, staying consistent—in school, at work, or at home—helps you build confidence.
3. **Learn from your mistakes.** Everyone falls short sometimes. What matters is what you learn when you get back up.

Daily Thought: Strength doesn't come from having it easy. It comes from moving forward when life is hard.

Principles 1, 2, and 12 from *The Thriver's Toolkit* tell you to:
- Turn tough times into chances to grow.
- Stay strong and focused, and don't give up when things go wrong.
- Work hard and stay dedicated.

CHAPTER 3

KINSHIP CARE—
A NEW KIND OF HELL

"If you're going through hell, keep going."
—*Winston Churchill*

"Alls my life I has to fight . . . but if God got us, then we gon' be alright."
—*Kendrick Lamar, "Alright"*

We rode in the police cruiser to the cousin's house who lived the next street over. I noticed that there were mostly single-family homes and only a few big buildings like the one we'd lived in. We showed the police officer where the house was, and he immediately pulled over. The yellow and green frame house towered over us. It looked like a mansion, and for a moment, I thought, *Everything is going to be OK.* We walked up to the screen door and when the officer knocked, an eyeball peered at us through the peephole. The door swung open.

I didn't know that I was entering Missouri's foster care system. I didn't know the system would be my "home" for ten years or more. I didn't know that we were four of about 13,000 kids in foster care in Missouri in 1982, part of a nationwide community of about 600,000 kids who are wards of the state. I didn't know that the State of Missouri now had legal custody over me and ultimate control over who would parent me. I didn't know that a government agency, the Division of Family Services, was now responsible for keeping me safe. And I didn't know that my appearance before a judge in the Curtis Jr. case would be the first of many court and child welfare appearances for this young boy.

In Missouri, the foster care system recognizes three types of placement: group homes, community homes, and kinship care, where you live with a family member. The state prefers for kids to go to kinship care because they think it will preserve important family connections. After all, who's more likely to take good care of a defenseless child—a relative or a stranger?

The woman connected to the eyeball in the door was a relative, but she was a stranger to me. I would later learn that she was Shirley, my mom's third cousin. Shirley didn't have any children of her own. As she swung the door open, I saw a massive human with huge hands and unbelievably large earlobes. An entryway large enough to double as a sitting room was behind her, where an old woman sat in a stained orange recliner.

I was hit with a strong stench as I walked from the kitchen into the dining room. The smell came from a bedside toilet sitting in that carpeted space. I was certain toilet water had splashed onto the floor. The stains and odor made it clear. This "bedroom-turned-dining-room" sat next to a small storage area that had once been a hair salon. Inside was an old, top-loading porcelain washer, now buried under piles of junk. In the years to come, I would get to know that washer well when I had to grip it for balance while being beaten across my backside.

On the second floor, there was a larger landing and hall, and Shirley's bedroom was at the back of the house. There was also a bathroom and a second and third bedroom, both of which were padlocked unless special guests arrived.

Within days, we were as settled in as well as we could be. I stood at the top of the stairs and heard my mom's aunt and uncle from Chicago talk to Shirley about what they should do with the four of us. I didn't know these people, and I was really confused by all the heated back and forth.

"How much is the state paying for these kids?" someone asked.

Another voice said, "It's not enough."

I shouted down, "I don't want to go with you anyway." I didn't know who I was talking to, and Shirley told me to shush.

"Stay out of grown folks' business," she called up the stairs. Those people left, and we only saw them once or twice more when we were a little older.

Shirley

Fear and loneliness were my constant companions. My brothers, sister, and I were the outcasts, second-class citizens among the favorite nieces and nephews. That island was about survival. And for whatever reason, Shirley treated me the worst. It was a very lonely place, and I've felt that loneliness my entire life.

I was abandoned, and I felt like I was in this life alone. I learned that foster kids are different. If you're a poor kid, at least you have your family looking after you. But foster kids are a lower class of poor kids. And I was more than a poor foster kid—I was a poor Black foster kid. I had nothing.

My fear of Shirley was unlike any fear I have felt since. It soon became clear that she organized the house into a perverse geography of pain. The first floor was for aggressive and violent shakes and attacks. The landing on the stairs was for sitting alone when we had been "bad." From there, the TV was impossible to see but impossible not to hear. I put my imagination to work and created images to go with the sounds for shows like *The Cosby Show*. The extra bedrooms on the second floor were used to store gifts Shirley had received over the years and for, as she would say, "beating the hell out of us." Nothing was worse than the bathroom.

"Strip and get your tail in that tub," she said as she drew water into the bath.

As soon as the water was up to my stomach, she'd come in with an extension cord. There was no place to hide as she violently swung the cord, welting my entire body as I sloshed around the water, trying to get away.

Mom had occasionally become overwhelmed and frustrated and had beat us, but it was nothing like how Shirley beat us, especially me. I never thought of Mom's beatings as abusive. When I think about my mom, what I remember is chronic hunger, abandonment, and neglect because of Curtis Jr., not malice.

But Shirley had malice, and she struck fear in me. She always seemed to be getting ready to beat us or recovering after beating us, so she could beat us again. She'd use those big hands to slap both sides of my face at the same time with all the force she could muster, like she was flattening a hamburger, which made my ears ring. If I wasn't clinging to the old washer on the first floor, she would make me strip naked in an extra bedroom and lie on the bed so she could beat me with a thick leather belt. It had a huge, shiny metal buckle, and it was painful. Each blow was like a little bit of death.

I'd get hit once, jump up instinctively, and Shirley would yell, "Get your tail down before I kill you!"

One time, my face was bashed in so badly that it felt like I'd been kicked in the face by a bull. On that day, I was sure she was going to kill me, and that was OK with me.

"Get your butt over here!" she screamed. I walked slowly into the guest room. "Lay across that darn bed," she yelled.

My body didn't even hit the mattress before the onslaught. I cried and begged, "Please, please, no more!"

Unable to get many words out between the strikes, I scurried across the bed to the other side so she couldn't reach me.

She let the slack out of the belt and screamed, 'Get your black butt back over here. I'm going to kill you, you worthless piece of trash. She swung the belt buckle and struck me on my chest. My body shook like the ground during an earthquake, and before I could see it coming, the belt buckle smashed me in the face. I fell to the floor as she came around the bed, still swinging the belt. I just lay there. I had no more fight in me.

Shirley didn't kill me that day, but she killed my will to live.

My chest had burst open and was bleeding. I could sense the sorrow from my brothers and sister. My mouth swelled up larger than a deformed baseball. I couldn't eat or speak well, and I drooled each time I opened my mouth. Shirley wouldn't take me to the doctor, but in a rare a moment of compassion, she gave me a sock filled with ice.

I nursed my wounds with that ice. When Sunday came around, her brother Ralph and sister-in-law came to visit. Ralph looked at my face and lashed out at Shirley, and they shouted back and forth.

Ralph said, "You are sick! What is this? Why haven't you taken him to the hospital?"

"If you want to take them, you can take them!" Shirley yelled back. "In fact, take them to live with you if you care so much."

That was the problem. No one cared—not Ralph or anyone else in the family wanted anything to do with us permanently broken kids.

My mouth was messed up for a while after that and was swollen shut for about a week. As the scar tissue began to form, so did my hatred of mirrors and posing for pictures. From then on, I hated looking at my reflection, and I couldn't wait to grow facial hair so I could mask the scar. I always had to sit on the passenger side of the school bus closest to the window so I'd be the only one who could see that scar reflected in the glass. Even as an adult, I've favor certain seats and positions in photos. It was all tied to that day, though that day was just one of many.

The abuse happened almost daily, and usually for no logical reason. As a result, my brothers and sister and I fought with each other as a coping mechanism, like prisoners often do. We tried to stay on Shirley's good side, which meant making sure that someone else was on her bad side.

When Shirley came home from church or somewhere else, we'd rush down the steps or bolt full steam from the kitchen—or wherever the old lady, Ora, had seated us to keep us from "messing" with each other. As soon as I heard her car muffler, a sense of dread fell over me. The car door would shut, and within a matter of seconds, the screen door would open, then the lock on the door would turn. Conditioned to do so, we 'd rush to the door and tattle on the others.

"Shirley, Antwon hit me," or "Orvin said a bad word," or whatever it was. We wanted to be on her good side. We knew that someone was getting beaten no matter what.

Ora would scream, "Shut up. Shut it up." Lifting her frail arm and pointing, Ora would single out who she thought was at fault that day.

Except for rare instances, like the day Ralph spoke up, or the time an anonymous neighbor reported Shirley, no one else did anything to acknowledge or stop the beatings. Shirley ruled by fear.

She liked my youngest brother the best, and I resented him for it. Most of the time, all four kids slept in the upstairs hallway on two mattresses. The three boys packed in the full-sized bed, with two on one end and one person in the middle. One night, I fell asleep and dreamed I was using the bathroom. When I woke up, I realized

I'd wet the bed. Afraid and trying to think of a way out of a beating, I looked over at my younger brother and thought, *Shirley really likes him.* So, I decided to pee on him and say that he had peed on me. That was the plan.

He woke up and yelled, "What are you doing? Are you pissing on me?"

I was caught. In the commotion, everybody woke up including Shirley. It was about 5:00 a.m., about the time we got up for school anyway. I got a beating for that one and had to sleep standing up all night for the next few days until, sometime later, I was allowed to sleep while sitting on a milkcrate. These were common forms of her punishment and torture.

On the days that I had to stand up to sleep, Shirley took the shade off the lamp, put the lamp behind us, and said, "Don't touch this lamp. Stand your butt right here."

We could see our shadows on her wall when we fidgeted, and could hear her say, "Stand your butt still."

The light reflected our shadows off the wall in Shirley's room, so she could check on us at any point in the night to ensure we were still standing.

Sometimes, it was my oldest brother and me. We figured out that if one of us stood really close to the light, it would cast a bigger shadow and hide the second person so that person could sleep. We took turns sleeping on the floor. Easing down to the floor was the hardest part because the floors creaked, and we didn't want to wake Shirley. Once when I was on shift, I fell asleep against the wall and slid all the way down to the floor. I woke to the smack of my face planting on the hardwood floor and felt Shirley tossing my body like a ragdoll and swinging that belt.

"You better not wake me again," she yelled at me. "And get your butt up," she yelled at my brother.

When I was "good," Shirley allowed me to sleep while sitting on the milkcrate. She'd give me a blanket that was itchy, but it was better than standing up all night. I'd prop myself up against the padlocked bedroom door and go to sleep. In the morning, my face would be smooshed from the door, my back and knees hurt, and I was often so very tired. I developed a wartime condition from this experience where I could fall asleep anywhere on demand.

On those days, I couldn't wait to get to school to sleep with my head resting comfortably on my arms on top of the desk. I couldn't focus, and often the teachers turned a blind eye, as if they knew my home life was complicated.

Memories of those years haunt me. I did my homework at the kitchen table. It was always so tense, especially when doing math. Shirley hovered over me, saying, "You'd better get the right answer."

If I didn't do it right the first time and had to erase it, she'd slap my hand with a thick ruler until it was red. And if I seemed distracted by her presence, she aggressively pushed my head into the books and gestured for me to focus on my work. I couldn't control my nerves, and I trembled as she loomed over me in the background, waiting to slap my hand if I got the wrong answer. It made it hard for me to think and process what was in front of me, and I fidgeted as if I was going to be struck for making any sound, even when she went in the other room.

Once, Shirley forced me to eat liver, which I hated. After eating it, I silently threw it up onto my plate. I couldn't help it. Then she made me eat my vomit and beat me.

She kept plenty of food in that deep freezer, but she was so strict. "No seconds," she would say after cooking my favorite, fried chicken. I swore at that time that I would never have more kids than I could feed.

The deep freezer was padlocked, and she carefully monitored the contents of the refrigerator and pantry. I was once beaten for stealing a piece of chocolate cake, but it was worth it.

One Christmas, I was given a coin bank that looked like a Tootsie Roll. There were a few dollars of coins in it, and I kept it at the base of the TV in the living room alongside family pictures. When I was punished, I'd sit at the bottom of the stairs and look at Shirley in her recliner, my resentment growing stronger every day. I imagined pushing past her, grabbing the Tootsie Roll bank, and running away and living off the coins.

One day I told her I was going to take my Tootsie Roll bank and run away, and she said, "Take it and get your Black butt out of here," gesturing toward the front door.

I wasn't brave enough to actually do it, but thinking about it comforted me on many days. There was no escape from Shirley.

After a while, my brother, Antwon, and I moved into the basement. It would periodically flood and have that mildew smell. The toilet smelled of sewer gas, and there was mold, but we didn't mind. Antwon stayed on one side, and I was on the other, islands unto ourselves, each of us in our own little place.

One day, Shirley was getting ready to beat Antwon, but he was done with it. An athlete who was physically fit and good with his hands, he screamed at her, "If you hit me, I'll mess you up!"

I took him at his word. My brother wasn't scared of anybody and ran with a rough crowd. Football saved his life by keeping him off the street. Shirley, likely thinking about this, took him at his word too.

"Stand right here, you damn fool. I'll be right back," she said. We both knew she was going to get the .22 caliber pistol. Antwon didn't stay. He grabbed a few things and left for good.

Depression

I had reasons to be depressed. My childhood was complicated. My mother had died at age 28, and I don't know if I knew that this wasn't normal. I'd never seen anyone die before, and since I didn't know how old you should be when you die, I thought I wouldn't live past 28 either. I struggled between my desire to live and my desire to die.

I often thought about what the world would be like without me in it. Shirley had killed my will to live, and I once made a plan to drown myself in the bathtub. My young mind wasn't developed enough to know that without a sedative or something that would paralyze me, I simply couldn't will myself to drown in a tub of water. When I was under the water, I held my breath and counted 1-1,000, 2-1,000, 3-1,000. But I always popped back to the surface by the time I got to 4-1,000.

I don't know if I really, deep down, wanted to kill myself. At least, that's what I told my therapist. When I told him that, he hugged me like I imagined being hugged by a father.

"What were you thinking?" he asked as I settled into his arms.

"I don't know if I was thinking," I whispered.

What I was feeling was pain. That pain has been a constant, and I suppose I really wanted to kill the pain, not myself.

In that brief moment of peace, he said, "Your life is valuable."

I don't know if I believed him. Other people had said the same thing, then put me back under Shirley's roof, but it was an optimistic seed.

Like for my brother, Antwon, the football field became a place to work out my feelings more constructively, but one day, I was hit from the back and took a bad fall. I was in terrible pain.

"Don't touch me!" I screamed as my teammates tried to lift me up.

I lay in the grassy field, looked up at the stars, and started to go numb. I thought this was it—death. I heard sirens, was braced by the paramedics, and lifted into the back of an ambulance. When I woke up, I was at Children's Hospital.

They'd cut off my uniform, and the doctors and nurses said, "You broke your hip and will need surgery."

They cut open my leg and put metal screws in my hip to hold it together, then stitched me back up. But the doctors and nurses also noticed Shirley's handiwork—the scars and welts that were all over my body and couldn't be explained away—the one I still have on my face, the one on my chest where it was split open by the belt buckle, and several dozen others from beatings on my backside, frontside, legs, and arms.

They asked me questions, and for the first time, I thought I'd be heard and helped. Finally, I broke open like a breached dam. Everything came pouring out through tears. I told them about the beatings, how Shirley kept the food locked away in that damned deep freezer, how she tormented me for being sexually abused and said that I'd invited and deserved it.

I told them I was afraid to go back, that I didn't want to go back. I was so scared, but these White people looked concerned, and they all promised they'd take care of me and told me my life was valuable.

Then, after some back and forth with the court system and case workers, they did what they said they wouldn't do—they sent me back.

When I returned home six weeks later, Shirley and I had a talk.

"You can take your butt to live in an orphanage," she said.

"I didn't tell them anything," I said. But they had too many details, details that Shirley denied but knew were true.

"So, you had to have talked," she said. "You can live in an orphanage where you'll be shuttled from facility to facility. You think living with me is tough? You'll be abused again," she said.

Shirley had put the fear of God in me about the orphanage. She described it as like being a prison, where the abuse was worse than anything I could imagine. So, I stayed with Shirley.

Now her abuse was different. It was better. She said things like, "You deserved to be sexually abused," and "You ain't gone be nothin," and, of course, "You're nothing—just stupid and worthless."

Later, I asked Shirley for a curl, a popular hairstyle, and she said, "No, but you can have a perm."

I got the perm, and she made me think it was close to a curl, particularly if I curled my hair with small rollers. Then she threatened to "send my soft butt to school in a dress." I got teased in school because boys didn't perm their hair. Shirley was delighted by that taunting. I later learned that this was emotional abuse. For a while after my hip surgery, I moved around in a wheelchair, then on crutches, and then I was back on my bicycle. Caseworkers visited us through the years to check in, but I learned not to trust them, so I was always "fine" when they asked how I was doing.

I don't think anyone from school knew exactly what was happening in our home, but they told me I was "special" from an early age. Just how special, I didn't know. Sometimes, they said, "Boy, you have a learning disorder." Other times I was told, "Boy, you have a behavior disorder." When I got into Stix, a magnet school in the city, I was told, "Stix is a school for gifted kids." I was confused.

From Stix, I went to Mason, a mixed-raced junior high. While at Mason, I found a friend at our church named Mr. Tillman. When I got in trouble at school for getting into a fight, there was no way I'd call Shirley. I knew she'd find out eventually, but I wanted it to be later rather than sooner. So, I called Mr. Tillman, and he came to school and spoke to the principal. Mr. Tillman understood me. He knew things weren't good at home, but despite his intercession, he couldn't stop me from being suspended.

For the next three days, I spent all my school time hanging out at a park. I'd get up, act like I was going to school, and get my bicycle I'd hidden the night before in the brush next to the house. I'd ride down the alley, coast downhill, and duck down when I passed my house, heart racing. I'd pedal like I was in a race for my life. When I got to the park, my heartbeat would slow down because I felt safe. I knew Shirley would never come to the park. She was obese and had other health problems that kept her close to home. Besides, she needed to be at the house to feed Ora, take her to dialysis, and empty her poo pot when I wasn't around to do it.

All day, I slept lying flat on the ground in the shade, walked around, and sometimes played basketball with other kids who'd ditched school or weren't in school anymore. And I rode my bicycle. It was three days of being a regular kid.

Uncontrolled Anger

I could have killed him. When I was thirteen years old, I got into an alley fight up the street. I was a troubled kid in many ways, and up to that point, I'd gotten into plenty of fights. But this was the first time I'd wanted to kill someone other than myself. I don't know why we were fighting, but I'm sure that it was nonsense and was agitated by the watching crowd.

The other kid was about my age but a little bigger, stronger, and faster. We both landed some blows and ended in a tussle. He was pinned down to the ground, and I straddled him. I had an out-of-body experience where I could feel the blood pumping through my veins. My thoughts were clouded, and my adrenaline was in overdrive. All I could think about was what this kid would do to me if I let him up. So, in one second, I grabbed a brick and held it over his head. In that same second, I asked myself, *What are we fighting for?* I don't know what came over me to think about ending that kid's life, but I'm glad I made a different decision. At that moment, I realized that I couldn't only ruin someone else's life but I could ruin my own. When I thought about it later, I knew that murder didn't fit with the life I wanted.

But it didn't take much to set me off, and I had a hard time controlling my temper, impulses, and life. I was over-sensitive. I thought that any threat, no matter how small, was meant to destroy me. I once hit a kid in the face so hard for stealing a fifty-cent bag of Chili-cheese Fritos I'd bought for a girl I liked. I'd worked hard for that money, but I didn't feel good after I hit him, not to mention that I shattered my writing hand. In a matter of seconds, it ballooned as much as his forehead. His face was unrecognizable—just like mine when Shirley hit me in the face with the belt buckle. I didn't like hitting this kid, but I felt like he didn't respect me. He took my chips, which were my currency with this girl, and that was a slippery slope.

Work for What You Want

The first and only game console I ever owned was an Atari that I bought around 1985. I'd saved more than $100 by working odd jobs. I set a goal to purchase it, and I did. At the start of my eighth-grade year, I bought an Adidas suit with my own money. It was the coolest outfit I'd ever owned, and it helped me gain some coolness and acceptance from my peers. I'd never had cool clothes or shoes before.

I worked and did whatever I could to earn money. When I worked, it meant I could eat when I wanted. Instead of sleeping in on snow days, I shoveled snow. I got up early, bundled up in sweatpants and jeans, used socks for gloves, and knocked on doors.

When asked, "Baby, how much do you charge?"

I always said, "Maim (it was mostly women who answered the doors), whatever you can spare is fine."

Some would take advantage of me and only give me five dollars to shovel what looked like a football-length staircase and sidewalk. Others would be more generous, so it always worked out. By noon, I had a pocket full of money. I was a saver, so I loved how my pocket bulged and how I felt after two back-to-back snow days, which were rare. I liked having money.

I also cut grass during the summer. I made a deal with Mr. Wallace down the street. He lived by himself, but his mother and sister lived within two doors.

"Mr. Wallace," I said, "I will cut your grass for free if you allow me to use your lawnmower to cut Mrs. Jackson's house and some others."

He agreed, and we shook on it.

I also spent long, hot days turning soil and pulling weeds to prepare for planting new seeds. Mr. Wallace's mother had a garden in her backyard, and he paid me to work in it sometimes. It was backbreaking work.

One summer, Shirley introduced me to a man named Mr. Weeden. He owned a construction company and a daycare, and he let me shadow him as a favor to Shirley. We took long trips on the highway to pick up supplies. Mr. Weeden sometimes fell asleep, and then he'd wake up all excited.

"Mr. Weeden, are you OK?" I softly asked when I thought he'd fallen asleep.

I didn't want to startle him, but I had to do something to wake him up because the speedometer was nearing 70 mph. With Mr. Weeden, I carried wood to other workers and cleaned up junk. Once, we had to tear down a penny candy store. To my surprise, it was dark, musty, and wet when we went in, but there was still some candy there.

"Take all you want," Mr. Weeden said. And I did. I filled my pockets and belly.

I worked hard whenever I could. Sometimes, I didn't get paid with money, but one of my customers said, "Stop by anytime you need a sandwich." Someone else took me to a local thrift shop to get some clothes. And they were better than the clothes we found in the alley! I also got clothes and food from the church.

Other forms of my good deeds paid off too. I was once chased by a group of gang members, and I stepped into a ditch and hobbled while I was running. I could see Mr. Wallace coming down the street as quickly as he could with his pistol in tow. I ran past my house to his porch while he shouted, "You stupid thugs leave this kid alone!" while pumping his pistol in the air. When the coast was clear, I hobbled home, went to the emergency room, and learned that I had broken my foot.

St. Edwards King Catholic Church was where we worshipped and went to vacation Bible school. I served as an altar boy and helped the priest during Mass, and sometimes I worked there. One summer I worked with Mr. Tillman in a program (the man the school called when I was in trouble). It was designed to keep us kids off the streets. It was when the Bloods and Crips were on the rise. At that time, gang violence, crack cocaine, and teenage pregnancy were all the talk. The church wanted us to avoid all of that.

One of the neighborhood kids I knew from school (he'd been a part of the group that chased me) couldn't have been thirteen years old, but he drove by us in his car while we were cleaning the church lot. He strutted out in his dope man shoes, the classic Nike Cortez shoes made popular by its association with gang culture and frequent appearance in hip-hop songs. He glanced over at us and chuckled, but he was eventually sent to prison.

A typical conversation among us kids was about who was murdered or who was in jail. Not far from us, someone had recently "gotten their head blew off." We saw the blood-stained concrete that never seemed to fade. I had to watch my back because I wasn't a part of a gang.

I didn't have time to join a gang. On Saturdays, I volunteered at the church. We met early to go to our hometown grocer called Schnucks, where I had my first W-2 job, and we collected expired pastries, bread, and other food items. I cherished those Saturdays, packing boxes for some elderly neighbors on my block and keeping one for myself. Carrying as much as I could down the alley for half a mile, I visited neighbors and distributed treats before I went home and heated up the pastries. I ate until I was full. We could also browse through donated clothes on Sundays after Mass and choose what we wanted.

During my freshman year in high school, I was bussed to the Academy of Math and Science. In high school, the cool kids and upperclassmen got seats at the back of the bus. One day, I decided to sit in the back because there was no one to sit with up front. A tall, scrawny upperclassman with nice clothes and shoes got on the bus, and he shot me a disapproving and aggressive look.

"Yo punk butt needs to move out of my seat," he said, pointing and laughing at my second-hand clothes and shoes. I ignored him and acted like he wasn't talking to me. It was the first week in school; he couldn't be talking to me.

"If you sit back here tomorrow, I'm going to beat yo butt," he said.

He had mistaken me for someone else as he dapped his friends, who continued laughing and egging him on. My friend from the neighborhood, Cornelius, was on the bus and was sitting up front. I wondered if it came down to a fight if Cornelius would help me. If the role was reversed, I knew I'd help him.

The next day, I had to sit in the back. Otherwise, I'd have problems with bullies from that point on. *May as well put an end to this stuff*, I thought. To my surprise, nothing happened. But a few days later when I felt comfortable and relaxed, we pulled to the front of the school, I grabbed my backpack and stood up. Then, I felt it. His fists rained down on me, one after the other, and I retreated into a sitting and ducking position.

"Stop it!" the bus driver yelled as he radioed for help.

I immediately regained my composure, lunged, and wrapped my arms around the other kid to stop the blows. Then, I beat his butt. One blow after another, I didn't stop even though I was tired. It went well beyond whipping him and defending myself. I wanted to send him and all the others a message. I was in a rage and out of control and went crazy on this kid until the bus driver pulled me off him. I was bloody, but so was he. I hadn't seen his fists coming, but he saw all of me coming at him.

The school security guard escorted me to the nurse's office and then to see the principal. I got an in-school suspension, and the school counselor introduced me to an older mentor from the community and some other upperclassmen boys. The rumor mill swirled, and I got the daps from everybody for defending myself. Cornelius hadn't helped me, but that was OK because that other kid never looked my way again.

I didn't have many problems after that because everyone knew I could hold my own, and they were smart enough to leave me alone. *Message delivered*, I thought. That was the second-to-last time I felt I needed to fight with my hands. What I needed to learn was how to fight with my mind.

Several years later, after hip surgery, many fights, broken bones, and emotional abuse, I got off the school bus and heard what I thought was our house alarm. I saw the rotating lights of an ambulance, and I frantically ran up the block. I couldn't imagine what could be wrong. I jumped the ledge into the yard, ran up to the front porch and through the door, and was met by a stunning sight.

Shirley, that powerful, towering woman, was lying on the floor immobile, unresponsive, and not so powerful.

"Do you have the code to the house alarm?" the paramedic asked.

Of course, I didn't. Shirley would never trust us with the code to the house alarm, and if she saw me messing with it, she would slap the hell out of me. So, no, I didn't know the code, but I'd seen her enter it so many times that I'd memorized the pattern. I started stabbing methodically at the box, and finally, I hit the right numbers and the alarm stopped.

Smoke had filled the house and set off the alarm. Shirley ate a lot of fried food, and apparently, she'd passed out while frying something. Luckily, the alarm brought first responders to the house quickly enough to turn off the stove before the house caught on fire. As they placed her on the stretcher and rolled her out the door, her eyes were open, but she couldn't speak.

Two or three weeks earlier, three of us kids had been home alone. When we heard Shirley's car arrive, we straightened up in a hurry and frantically got back into the places where Shirley had told us to stay. We listened for the usual noises. First, the car door would open, and it did. Second, the screen door would creak open, but that didn't happen, and we couldn't hear her key in the lock. We waited, frozen by fear in our places, and wondered if she was trying to catch us doing something so she could cuss us out.

After what seemed like hours, I looked out the window. I saw Shirley's car and what I thought was a leg on the ground, but the retaining wall in the front blocked my view. It was cold and icy outside, so we thought Shirley may have fallen. We were afraid to open the door because Shirley would "beat our Black butts," so we waited. We couldn't use the phone. She had most things rigged so she could tell if we messed with it. After a while, we unlocked the front door to get a closer look. Shirley was on the ground, and we helped her to her feet and into the house. Afterward, we never talked about it. We assumed she'd slipped and hit her head.

"So, what's wrong with her?" I asked the paramedic.

"I'm not sure. Probably an aneurysm," he answered.

"What's an aneurysm?" I asked.

"It's when a blood vessel pops in your brain," he said.

I knew her situation was serious. I asked if I could go to the hospital and hopped in the ambulance. Shirley was admitted and was taken to surgery. It was strange to see her lying alone at the mercy of tubes and machines and strangers.

"It was a stroke," they said.

The stroke didn't kill her, but she'd never come home again.

"Shirley is incapacitated," the social worker later told us.

I wondered if her earlier fall had something to do with it or if the fall was an early warning sign. I didn't know.

For several months after that, my brothers and sister and I lived in the house by ourselves. Church members brought us food, and we ate fried chicken, baked ham, and turkey—and we ate all we wanted.

But one day, social workers showed up and said we couldn't live alone anymore. We heard that Shirley's sister had called the Division of Family Services, who researched our relationships and found a different home for each of us.

I moved up the street to my best friend's grandmother's house—Ms. Jackson's. She was a good woman. She had a daughter two years younger than me and a grandson, who was probably a year younger but in one grade higher. They lived with her. He was my best friend. During summer, we'd wake early and be outside playing football, court (a game similar to stickball), and basketball. The milkcrate hoop was nailed to a tree in the alley. We played there, trying not to twist our ankles on the uneven pavement while using the base of the tree as an explosive launch pad to dunk the ball. If you hit the tree just right to catapult yourself into the air, you felt like an NBA player, screaming "and one" with the slightest tap. When I'd been allowed to sleep over, we were up all night playing video games and eating late-night egg sandwiches smothered in butter or huge bowls of cereal.

I thought that moving up to Ms. Jackson's would bring more of those good times, but I lived with them for less than six months. When the state had to decide about my permanent placement, they asked if I wanted to live with Ms. Jackson. I said no. She was willing to have me, but I wasn't willing to stay.

Her daughter had once said to me in the heat of an argument, "At least I have a mom."

She knew about my mother's death. She knew I didn't have anyone who cared about me, and her words devastated me. So, when they asked if I wanted to stay with them, I said no. I'd rather be around people who couldn't say things like that to me. I know we were kids, and she didn't know what she was saying, but I'd already lived a life of trauma.

This time, I'd choose my own trauma, not have it forced on me. I chose to go to an orphanage, Annie Malone Children's Home. It was lonely, but I got to choose. I would do what I needed to do to take care of myself.

Tools You Can Use:

Sometimes people you love can't give you what you need. That can hurt deeply, but it can also teach you how to love yourself better.

1. **Don't let anger run your life.** It's okay to feel mad or sad but holding on too long can keep you stuck.
2. **Find people who lift you up.** A friend, mentor, or coach can help you find hope again when you feel alone.
3. **Let go so you can grow.** Forgiveness isn't saying what happened was okay—it's saying you're ready to move forward.

Daily Thought: The moment you stop carrying old pain, your hands are free to reach for something better.

Principles 4, 5, and 15 from *The Thriver's Toolkit* tell you to:

- Forgive others and let go of old hurt to move on.
- Build and lean on a strong support team.
- Be mindful and calm, especially when life feels heavy.

CHAPTER 4

ORPHANAGE

*"I don't know what God has planned for me or you or anyone,
but I do know that in darkness, you discover an indistinguishable light."*
– Cory Booker, United States Senator

"I got loyalty, got royalty inside my DNA."
—Kendrick Lamar, "DNA."

After Shirley's illness, I tried to figure out how to control my anger. I was still a kid who exploded when things got bad, and my angry reactions showed a main weakness that left me open to blame and punishment that came with those outbursts. I would get so angry that I would shake like my first car did when I opened her up on the highway and had to hold tightly to the wheel to keep control of it.

I often asked myself if my explosiveness had helped me in any way. And I realized that I couldn't become my own enemy. I didn't like who I was when that part of me was triggered, and I knew I needed to take control. Most people don't want to be around others who are easily set off and unpredictable, and I needed to control myself.

I found out that aggression and passion have similar features but different outcomes. Aggression is uncontrolled and pushes people away, but passion uses that same emotion more productively. I learned to harness aggression and anger and turn them into productive passion, which helped me become a better person. Passion inspires hope, but aggression inspires fear.

I made it a habit to speak slowly and put others first in conversation, so I could turn my aggression into passion. Then I could communicate clearly and honestly and build connections that lifted up those around me. Even though my kindness was sometimes misunderstood as weakness, I found the inner strength to stay calm without reacting impulsively.

I decided that if I wasn't in a life-or-death situation, I could simply not say anything. Instead, I could think and slow things down because most situations aren't life or death. I had to be careful because when I felt attacked, my first words in a heated moment weren't words of life but words meant to cause that same pain to the other person. So, I became quick to think and slow to speak.

"The only thing you control in any exchange is your reaction," my therapist said. "You can't always control how it makes you feel or what it makes you think, but you can control your reaction." I learned that I should try to build others up, not tear them down, and sometimes, "you just have to remove yourself" from a situation, as my therapist said.

Those words helped me leave Ms. Jackson's home. Her daughter's words had hurt me and rather than hurting her back, I knew it was best for me to leave so I wouldn't be in that situation again. And by building others up, I could grow connections. In other words, aggression used the right way could be a powerful tool to inspire.

Learning about my main triggers helped me handle heated conversations ahead of time and manage my surroundings. Knowing my triggers let me take moments to think, to get different perspectives, and to pay attention to an uplifting inner voice instead of the one that said, "Don't take mess from nobody."

With slower responses and having a generous attitude in my conversations, I started to listen to truly understand, which was good for the other person and me. I didn't react out of raw emotion but toward engaging with mindful enthusiasm. Then I could influence others to see, think, or act differently.

It's a hard thing, for sure, when you're a small boy and you realize that you have to take care of yourself if you want to survive. It's easy to lose hope when you have limited options based on your age and stage in life. It's easy to lose hope when you don't have any control over your life.

Self-control Is the Key

Today, we see kids and adults who can't control themselves. They get really upset over small things. They feel like they can't control what happens around them, their future, or their country. Some think they're victims. When people think there aren't enough opportunities or when they disagree about money, race, and politics, many people make bad choices. We've become a country where people blame others for their problems instead of taking responsibility for themselves.

Each of us needs to take charge of own selves and our feelings. That's the first step to having more control over what happens around you. You're responsible for you. I'm responsible for me. We should all be held accountable when our negative behavior hurts others.

It took me a long time to understand this because I didn't have a strong foundation for knowing right from wrong. I only knew that you were either the victim or the person hurting others. This happened either by choice or by chance.

I was really hard on myself. Even though I was naturally kind as a kid, I worried that others might think I was weak. Being abused early in life made me be very careful around people. I often pulled away from relationships so I wouldn't get hurt. I felt self-conscious about how I looked, especially my scar. These feelings were hard to get over because I couldn't stop the negative thoughts in my head. When I thought someone might hurt me, I'd get too defensive. This made me lonely, and I was mean to myself and others.

To fix this, I had to figure out what set me off. Here are some of them:

- Not having control or choices (like when I was a kid)
- Taking timed tests
- Feeling like people are using me
- Being threatened or bullied (or thinking that I was)
- Worrying that my kindness made me look weak
- Getting upset when things weren't fair
- Wanting to protect people I care about when they're hurting

Understanding that these are triggers still helps me today. It's important to know what sets you off so you can deal with it.

Growing up with violence made me violent too. To survive, I had to be as intense as everyone else around me. I saw others lose their temper, so I did too. I saw others break into homes, so I broke into a home. I did these things because I thought they were my only options. When my mom died, I felt like I had no control over anything. Years later, when my brother got paralyzed, it reminded me that I was only one bad choice away from the life I was supposed to have—the life of a poor, Black, street kid. I had to think carefully about what I was doing.

Despite everything I'd heard about orphanages, I decided to go to the Annie Malone Children's Home. I was fifteen when I split up from my brothers and sister for good. My case worker said my younger brother went to the Emergency Children's Home (ECHO). That would later be my last group home as a foster kid. I wasn't sure, but I think my sister went to Marian Hall, a home for girls only. After that, she moved around to several other homes. She even stayed with me at Annie Malone for a while.

When I went into residential care, I felt like I'd sunk deeper into the worst part of America. Shirley had made this feeling worse and took away any hope I had for something better. I saw myself as a kid from the gutters. My parents didn't think much of themselves, and I was the same way. Inside me, there were two voices that fought each other. One voice told me I was "less than" everyone else and didn't deserve parents, love, or anything good—even if God offered it to me directly. The other voice held onto a tiny bit of hope. It wanted meaning, connection, and a place to belong.

I was embarrassed to tell my friends from school that I'd moved to an orphanage and that I had no family. I felt guilty, like I'd done something to deserve this, or that maybe Mom had died because of me. I was angry that I didn't have parents to do things with me like normal kids did. Most of all, I was scared. I was afraid that I'd end up like my parents—poor and not ready for life's challenges—and that no one would ever love me.

My brokenness wasn't my fault. I didn't make any of the decisions that led to my traumatic experiences. I had to accept this truth, so I could get through the darkness of the days and nights after Shirley left. *We're children, and we have to depend on the adults in our lives*, I told myself over and over. The more I said it, the more I thought I'd believe it. And then I wouldn't feel shame, guilt, or fear about being judged—all feelings I'd had to deal with. I knew I had to act differently to succeed in this place. That was fine because I'd been practicing self-control for a while now.

I stuffed my plastic bags, said goodbye to the Jacksons, and loaded everything into the social worker's car. By now, I'd lost everything. Every important relationship, no matter how messed up, was gone. As I made the 2.5 mile trip to the Annie Malone Children's Home, I knew I was about to enter a new world.

The Orphanage

The Annie Malone home is in the heart of a neighborhood that was the historical home of St. Louis's Black middle class. I didn't know what middle class was, but it looked like more people lived in houses—and, to me, that always meant that they had food. Like the neighborhood I came from, this one had solid brick homes that lined the streets. Some were single-family houses, some were two- or four-family apartments, and most had been built in the first twenty or thirty years of the nineteen hundreds. But they were showing their age. Weeds covered some empty lots, and some buildings looked like they were about to fall down. But as we turned north onto Annie Malone Drive, an amazing brick building appeared ahead of us. It looked like a mansion to me, and it covered almost a whole block.

"Wow," I said, "it looks like that house on television." I was talking about the White House. It had four big white columns that held up a roof over the entrance. I couldn't believe that this was about to become my new home. *The people who own that home must be rich*, I thought. At this point, I knew I'd have to work even harder to make it.

There was an early 1900s institution in this neighborhood called Poro College, just a short walk from my new home. Poro College was the first headquarters of Poro Beauty Products. The company sold products to the nation's growing African American community, which could afford hair-straightening and other beauty products.

Life was easier with "good hair," and the Poro company's hair straightening product made life a little bit easier for African American women with "bad hair." But the only way to get the product was to have a little extra money to spend. Clearly, a large number of African American people with some money were living not only in St. Louis but also across the country. Otherwise, companies like Poro wouldn't have succeeded. Annie Minerva Turnbo Pope Malone, the person with the vision behind Poro College and its successful line of hair care products, understood this. It made her one of the most unlikely millionaires in history. My new home was named for her.

Annie Turnbo was born in Metropolis, Illinois. She was orphaned as a child and raised by her older sister. She had nine siblings. Annie had a talent for chemistry and watched what her African American community needed. She invented her famous hair-straightening product. In 1902, she moved to St. Louis and grew her business by hiring salespeople to sell products door-to-door. At the 1904 World's Fair, she sold her products and started her national expansion. In 1914, she married Aaron Malone and became a Black female millionaire within four years. She built Poro College with a training facility and company headquarters. The college employed around 200 local people at its peak and became a source of community pride. It also hosted the National Negro Business League's headquarters. When a tornado hit in 1927, the American Red Cross used the college as a relief center. Poro College went beyond beauty training and offered courses in literature, drama, and music to give a complete education.

By the 1950s, the training model Malone created at Poro College had expanded to 32 branches nationwide. Her business and fortune continued to grow. She moved the business to Chicago in 1930, but she never forgot St. Louis or what it felt like to be orphaned at a young age. One of the many charities she supported was the St. Louis Colored Orphans Home, which sheltered the many homeless

African American children who wandered the streets without care. In 1901, the St. Louis Colored Orphans Home moved to a new location, but by 1919, it had been condemned.

That year, Annie Malone became president of the home's board of directors. She not only moved it to a new location and saved it from going bankrupt, but she also used its closeness to Poro College to make it a year-round cultural heart for the community. Its Christmas parties for the orphans were legendary. In the late 1930s, a Stowe Teachers College sorority, the Girl Scouts, the Brownies, the University City Chauffeur's Club, and the DeMun Avenue Community School all joined in to give the kids gifts and holiday celebrations.

Three years after her time as board president ended, she gave $10,000 of Poro profits to buy the land for a new Black orphanage building. At that time, Annie Malone's business empire was at its peak. When the new St. Louis Colored Orphans Home was dedicated as the Annie Malone Children's Home in 1946, it continued the original home's traditions of community participation and support. The Annie Malone May Day Parade is still held in downtown St. Louis.

As we pulled up in front of the Annie Malone Home, I said to myself, *One day, I'll own a home like this, maybe in a community like this.*

I walked between those big white columns and through the front door with all my belongings and trash bags full of clothes. At the first checkpoint, the social worker said to the attendant, "Orvin Kimbrough, permanent placement."

We walked down a hallway to check in with the woman who would become one of my counselors, Mrs. Heron. I didn't say much.

"How are you, Orvin?" she asked.

"I'm fine," I said.

I wasn't fine. I was afraid, and I was angry at Shirley's family because none of them cared enough to take us. *I don't have anyone*, I thought as I looked around at the massive building, now my new home.

After check-in, someone took me up the big staircase. On the second-floor landing, I could see that the building was split in two—the north and south halves looked exactly the same. I would live in the North Dorm, while the younger kids, later including my little sister, lived in the South Dorm. The living areas were along the stairs on either side, with a small bathroom off each, where the children showered together from one shower head. The dorm rooms were split into east and west rooms, each with up to six beds. The floor had black and white tiles arranged like a chess board, and small closets held whatever belongings we had. Each room had a bell in it, which would ring when it was time to change activities—go to class, go to art class, eat—and an intercom system made announcements.

I continued up to the third floor. The first room to the left was for me and my roommate. A window looked out over the play-ground, and that's where we'd sit and watch the younger kids running around and wait for our turn to go out. The groups rarely mixed together. The closet was bigger than on the second floor, and we had separate shower stalls. But the bells were still there, showing the loving control Annie Malone would have over my life.

For the first time, I had to live by a point system that connected levels and privileges with behavior. Level three was the highest honor and gave you the chance to go on home visits if you had a "resource," the clinical term for someone in the community willing to take you for a weekend, do outdoor activities, work, or watch TV.

"The goal of the point system, Orvin," my therapist said, "is to help kids learn acceptable behaviors and to have a direct feedback loop to rewards and consequences."

I hated that damn system. It did two things well: when kids were obedient and followed the rules, all was good, but when children had small rule breaks, they were sometimes made worse because all we could understand was what they were taking away from us. It was easy to fall into despair and not care about the points at all. *If they were going to take points away from us, then let's really earn the punishment and give 'em hell*, we thought.

While I was basically a good kid and tried to stay at the higher level, I was still a teenager. Within days, I got into a fight with a boy named Jimmy, a hothead who would later show a tender, compassionate side. This was my first fight at Annie Malone and the last fistfight of my youth. As boys, we were moody, and a lot of that was simply because of our developmental, hormonal stage. A lot of the other kids I remember were girls. There were the Robinson sisters; Clarisa, who went to Turner Middle School; the short, fair-skinned April (who caught the bus with me) who was heading for independent living; and many others who stayed a short while or longer.

I had noticed girls, like the brown-skinned CC. When I lived with Shirley, she'd liked my friend Ronell. He and I once got into a fight. CC's light-skinned, heavier cousin, Pat, liked me, and she used to knock on Shirley's door to see if I could come out to play.

I was always hesitant. I didn't want to play because her body reminded me of a shorter, light-skinned Shirley, and she was fast. She more sexually advanced—*downright promiscuous*, I thought. I'd learned a lot about the intense feelings that led to sex, but I didn't want to have sex because I was afraid that she'd get pregnant. So, I'd go back to my basement room in Shirley's house and touch myself. I'd get a rush and think to myself, *Boy, that felt great!* I had to hand wash the sock along with my other clothes.

I was somewhat of a late bloomer when it came to acting on my desires with girls, at least compared to the kids I hung out with. To hear them tell it, everybody was "getting some," except me. I was too afraid of the disease that seemed everywhere—pregnancy. This terrified me.

At Annie Malone, the girls were always around. When they walked into the room, you couldn't help but look and have your hormones go crazy, but you had to be careful because the source of your erection—I mean affection—could be someone's sister. You never knew.

It was constant teenage teasing. Once, I let on that I liked the girl who rode the bus with me, April. When she walked into the kitchen area with other girls, Jimmy—who could be a hyper, fun-loving kid—jumped up, put his arm on my shoulder, pointed in her direction, and in his loving and intense way said, "There she is, go say something."

"No, Jimmy," I said, scooting down in the seat.

"You're a punk," he said.

I looked in April's direction and tried to ignore Jimmy's taunts.

He could barely get the words out because he was laughing so hard, but he shouted, "Orvin likes you, April!"

I didn't think I'd recover from that. But I did recover, and I did like her. Like me, like Jimmy, she had an optimistic sadness. She was even better company at the bus stop now that she knew I liked her.

Jimmy always said something to make me uncomfortable. Once when I was in the shower chasing that feeling (you know, the feeling, the one that was typically in a sock), I heard someone walk in, pause by my stall, and burst into laughter. I didn't know who it was until I came out and into the TV room, only to see Jimmy sitting on the couch, staring as if he'd caught me doing something terrible.

"I saw you," he said in front of the other boys.

"Saw me?" I said. "Saw me doing what?"

He said matter-of-factly, "You know what," pointing and laughing. "Playing with yourself," he said.

I answered, "If you were watching me in the shower, we should all be laughing at your nasty butt."

Everyone laughed at Jimmy and he got mad, but I didn't care. He was now the target of the joke that he'd started. I knew I wasn't the only kid on the planet who'd figured out how to reward myself for good behavior, for not messing with the girls.

Together, all these kids and I formed a community of kids who understood the pain and uncertainty of life in the foster care system. I had a good group of people watching out for me at Annie Malone. There was Mr. Robinson, my young, African American house parent. He went on to become a director at the YMCA, and I'm still in touch with him today. Annie Malone had a basketball court out back, and I spent a lot of time there, watching the best, most explosive players prove how good they were and score points on and off the court. Our basketball hero was Mr. Trice, who had a deadly three-point shot, and Mr. Robinson, who could hold his own. They also talked serious trash as they played against us kids. Together, these people became a sort of family to me. They gave me the consistency and predictability that I craved, and they tried to make Annie Malone as homelike as possible.

The tradition of holiday celebrations that had begun decades before continued while I was there. Sometimes, adults from the community brought us gifts. At Christmas and Thanksgiving, the home filled with the smell of turkey, gravy, and all the fixings. At times, we would go on outings to places like the YMCA, the Boys & Girls Club, and the Muny, the outdoor municipal theater in Forest Park. I went to my first St. Louis Cardinals game while at Annie Malone. We sat all the way at the top of Busch Stadium and were allowed to order one hot dog and one soda. We always traveled as a group in the white van with the name "Annie Malone" proudly displayed. Of course, I was self-conscious about people looking at us wherever we went, but it didn't matter. We were happy to be out seeing the city, stopping at Schnucks for a late-night snack run, and enjoying as normal a life as we could.

But being "like a family" isn't "being a family," and an institutional structure isn't family structure. In a true family, the members are always around, not just around when their shifts start. At Annie Malone, there were two or three shifts. You had the night workers who worked eight hours. Their main job was to make sure we woke up on time.

"Get up," we heard each morning, "lights on."

We would get up, shower, and go down to the kitchen to eat where there was plenty of food. Then we went out the door to catch our buses.

Then there were the day workers. They were around for those of us who either didn't go to school or got in trouble at school. The day workers also took us to various outside therapy appointments, medical appointments, and court visits.

Finally, the after-school workers made sure we were fed, did homework, got our meds, and were in bed by a certain time.

"Lights out," we'd hear from the television room.

In normal families, like that of my best friend Ronell, you could go to family members for anything, at any time. And his grand-mother, Ms. Jackson, was the boss. At Annie Malone, it wasn't that simple. In most cases, we had scheduled time, and then there were policies and procedures, as well as state workers and agency staff, who were all part of the team that made decisions that affected me. With all those people involved, it seemed like no one was really in charge there.

I began to dream about two-parent families. I loved it when I would see a White "resource." I didn't know why, but they were mostly White. Both the husband and wife would pick up my room-mate, keep him for the weekend, and then drop him back off. He told me stories of what he'd done.

"I got to swim. We watched movies. We went to the park. We went to Six Flags," he said.

This is what two-parent families do, I thought. They have fun. I thought that I might get adopted. But I felt like I was simply grow-ing older during the days, weeks, and months that I stayed at Annie Malone, not really being helped to grow or nurtured. I was always curious about the different personalities and jobs of these resources.

"She stays at home, and he does something in business," my roommate said.

Still, my Annie Malone family did its best, and they cared for us. But did they love us? Maybe. But not how a parent loves a child. Parents punish children to help them grow, but in institutions, counselors punish children for breaking rules. The discipline of a parent is personal and fits their child's needs and values, while institutional punishment is the same for everyone and applies broadly within the system. Parents, driven by emotional bonds, can be flexible, while caregivers in institutional settings aren't influenced by such bonds. Parents are flexible; institutions are consistent.

At Annie Malone, rule-breakers and rule-followers were mixed together. I thought some kids were there because they misbehaved and broke the law, while kids like me simply didn't have parents. I felt like a victim of my situation, unlike many of my peers who were victims of their own choices. My resentment and anger grew as I thought about kids who had advantages but still ended up there. Why leave your own family? Today, my perspective has changed.

Despite the structure Annie Malone gave, there was a lot of fear, too. The people I mentioned were wonderful, but there were a lot of adults going in and out that I didn't know; there were too many "anybodies" around. For a kid raised in constant fear of adults, known and unknown, that was traumatic. Annie Malone successfully met my basic needs like food, water, safety, and shelter, but didn't meet my emotional needs. Sometimes, in addition to my individual therapy, I went to group therapy, where we worked out our feelings toward each other and tried to understand our identity as growing boys. These were always awkward and shallow because we weren't sure of ourselves and lacked confidence. So even if we talked, they were never serious conversations. As a result, my serious nature increased while at Annie Malone.

I knew I was in a bad situation. I knew if I didn't make friends and have good relationships, I wouldn't have much of a life, and I didn't have a backup plan. So, for the most part, I decided to earn points and move up the level system, and I did what was expected of me. It had gotten easier for me because I'd worked on controlling my temper and on having an attitude that brought people closer to me instead of pushing them away.

Doing what was expected of me made some adults like me. Just like the years before when I worked odd jobs, I was rewarded if I worked hard for adults. I tried not to create problems, even though my life was full of problems. I had good relationships with house parents and counselors. These were the most powerful and successful people in my life; these were the people in charge. By not creating problems and making good relationships, I got privileges like being able to exercise and the freedom to go outside, on trips, to social activities, and to work.

And these people stuck up for me because I did what I was supposed to do. I didn't feel like I could make the mistakes most kids made, and if I did, I couldn't afford to get caught. The first time I saw prostitutes and crack cocaine up close, aside from some of my mom's friends and her drugs from far away, was in the orphanage. By now, I knew I'd been born in the wrong place, and I could understand how whole neighborhoods could develop hard hearts like mine. I lived in survival mode in a hard world where death was always around, not natural deaths, but early deaths from bad health, no access to doctors, violence, and drugs. Group homes didn't protect us from this. I was on an emotional roller coaster, but I tried not to show the people in charge how much hate was in me.

At times, I hated my mom for the childhood she gave me. I blamed her for dying the way she did, for not protecting me when I needed it most, for the many bad things in my life, and I blamed my dad for not being there too. My heart was filled with hatred and feeling sorry for myself. At one point, I decided that it was OK for me to fail because they let me down, they had failed me. And my heart grew harder.

But a hard heart creates bitterness that changes how people see you. It ruins your perspective, eats away at your being, and works against success. We can't give up on life because someone else failed to live it right. The bottom line is that we can't have a hard heart if we want to live into God's plan for us. And God has a plan for everyone, I learned when we went to Antioch Baptist Church up the road from the orphanage.

By now, my connection with my siblings was pretty distant. My sister came to Annie Malone, and just like that, she was gone. I had friends in my old neighborhood, where many kids lived with their mom, grandma, and, on rare occasions, both mother and father. But I didn't see them much once I went into the orphanage.

Years later, I learned that my best friend, Ronell, went to prison for something drug related. His cousin, Red, who lived with his mom in an amazing apartment with a pool, also faced a similar fate. Once, they dared me to jump into the pool's deep end, tap the bottom, and come back up. Even though I didn't know how to swim, I took the dare. When I sank, Ronell pulled me out of the water. That night, we ate well as usual and played video games, but we never talked about what happened. We'd been best friends when we were younger, as close as brothers. Knowing them and their family well, I believe that their lives would have taken a different turn if they'd had different social circles.

Luckily, I could still go to the Academy of Math and Science. I didn't like it when the bus dropped me off close to the orphanage. I tried to keep my new home a secret and asked the bus driver, "Please drop me at the other corner," when I got on the bus.

Ms. Kennedy, the school counselor, continued to be a rock for me. With her help, I started to find a place in the world. As a freshman and sophomore, I played basketball and wrestled. These were good outlets for me. Once, I got points taken away because I skipped group therapy so I could go to basketball practice.

I told my therapist, "If I don't practice, I don't play."

This was an example of how strict the rules were in an institution compared to how flexible a working two-parent household could be. I barely got any playing time because I wasn't a good player, but that wasn't the point.

During my first summer at Annie Malone, I worked for a landscape company. I got up early, packed a sandwich and plenty of water, and went to the pickup location to cut grass. I worked long days and left at dawn and returned to Annie Malone when it was almost dark. It exhausted me in so many ways. I got paid in cash, but the therapists at Annie Malone insisted that I turn my money over to them. I refused to let go of it. This led to consequences, but again, I didn't care because I didn't want them to control me any more than they already were.

The following year, the Academy of Math and Science closed, and I moved to Gateway Tech, a big school in a renovated tech school. At Gateway, I played basketball and ran cross-country, not by choice but as a condition to playing basketball. Gateway had a major advantage that shaped my life: it let students pick a major in subject areas like health careers, math, science, and performing arts. I chose physical therapy because it was a helping profession, and I had a chance to work with the great Erwin Claggett and the St. Louis University basketball team. Hanging out with the team exposed me to a lot of things I wouldn't have experienced otherwise, especially college life.

One of the big lessons from my sophomore year was getting kicked off the basketball team for eating a Blow Pop before a game.

Coach Bunche burst into the locker room, yelling, "Kimbrough, what's in your mouth?"

"A Blow Pop," I replied, looking at him confused.

It was obvious I had a Blow Pop in my mouth. *Is the coach OK?* I wondered. He told me to get dressed and quickly removed me from the team for breaking the rule of no-eating two hours before a game.

I was furious and looked at him as if he'd lost his mind. I wasn't the only one eating a Blow Pop, but he made me the example. So, I left the locker room and never returned. *The injustice*, I thought. Some of the other boys laughed at how ridiculous it was to get kicked off the team for breaking that rule and that I let myself get caught eating the Blow Pop. That was fine; it gave me more time to work.

Mrs. Kennedy took me to my first job interview with Rosa Grigsby, a Black woman at the Schnucks supermarket.

"She was the store manager," I said to Mrs. Kennedy in amazement. "Oh, by the way, I got the job!"

Mrs. Kennedy looked at me and smiled, as if the interview had been set up, as if she was the invisible hand.

I continued to have fights with the Annie Malone staff about turning over my paycheck, which had money taken out for state, federal, and union dues. *What the hell is all of this?* I thought. To make it worse, they wanted me to put the check into a checking account, and then they'd give me an allowance. I didn't know what a checking account was. I wanted my money where I could see it, like in that Tootsie Roll bank.

Within weeks of arriving at Annie Malone, I learned about the Independent Living Program. Independent living was temporary housing for teens in foster care. The agency had recently fixed up a huge building into other services and apartments for older kids. To qualify, I had to be at the agency for a certain amount of time, have the right attitude and be motivated, and be seventeen or eighteen. It was a competitive application process.

My case manager from the state gave me a tour of the building that had alarm systems, cameras, and locks on everything. Aside from the feeling of being caged, I remember thinking, *These are cool apartments*. More than just the apartments, I welcomed the freedom to come and go as I chose and the additional privileges I'd have if I was accepted into the Independent Living Program. My therapist thought that taking some life skills courses through the State of Missouri would be good preparation for independent living.

"Life skills?" I asked, confused.

"Yes," she answered. "You'll learn about checking, savings, budgeting, interviewing, getting an apartment, transportation—all the stuff that will help you live independently."

Finally, I'm going to learn about where they're putting my money, these so-called checking and savings accounts, I thought.

Life skills courses offered by the Division of Family Services were meant to prepare us for life after the group home. A cab picked me up and took me to a huge government building in downtown St. Louis. There, I joined other kids who lived in other group homes around town or were in kinship care. We completed exercises and answered discussion questions meant to help us know how to navigate the world. The life skill courses were good.

"These are things that most people learn by watching their parents," the instructor often said.

I learned how to function in society and work with banking, utilities, landlords, etc., but I also learned that when you meet someone, you need to look that person in the eye and give a firm handshake. It was a "sign of confidence" and the "language of business."

Business, I thought, *hmmm. That's what Annie Malone, the founder of the home, did; that's what some of the people in suits who come to visit Annie Malone do. Business is what the neighborhood I live in was known for in its heyday!*

This was a huge discovery for me: just by looking someone in the eye, shaking hands, projecting my voice, and speaking clearly,

I could make people think I was a confident person. I couldn't believe it at first and felt awkward when I first tried it. These skills didn't come naturally to me, but the more I practiced, the better I got at it, and my self-confidence improved a lot.

And sometimes people would tell me, "You have some good leadership skills."

I didn't know what that meant, but I got involved with the newly created Foster Care Youth Advisory Board with Mrs. Thomas. She was a director with the Division of Family Services. That year, we visited the state capital and argued for an increase in our clothing allowance. It was amazing. We succeeded in our argument, and our annual clothing allowance was raised from $150 to $200. That number hadn't changed in over a decade, and this was a proud moment. *I did that*, I thought.

Foster Care Realities

The truth of my situation started to sink in. I wasn't going to be adopted. I was too old by this point. People were more likely to adopt babies and small kids.

I could finish high school, but it would be hard because I was worried about what lay ahead without a family. *How am I going to take care of myself?* I wondered. I was old enough to understand how serious my situation was, and I was frozen with insecurity.

The statistics for kids in foster care, whether kinship care, group home, or community living, are not good. An average of 61 percent of children who enter the foster care system test positive for developmental delay just like I did. Twenty-four percent of foster youth struggle with disabilities in school just like I did. Across the United States, 52 percent of foster youth attend schools that rank in the lowest 3 percent just like I did.

According to the Promise2kids site, about 50% of foster kids will earn their high school diploma. Only 10% of former foster youth attend college, and out of that 10%, only 3% graduate. Further, around 50% of former foster youth are homeless within the first two years after leaving foster care; roughly 60% of girls get pregnant within a few years; 50% of those who leave foster care are unemployed; 33% receive public assistance.

I didn't want that to be me.

Before my life skills classes, I didn't know the statistics, but I sensed that my options were limited. If I'd known all these statistics growing up, my self-worth would have been even lower than it was. The problem was that the people who did know how badly these statistics reflected on foster kids sometimes let the numbers lower their expectations for us. For example, a lot of people expected me to do exactly what my parents had done. They didn't expect me to overcome and achieve success. They expected me to simply get by and join the ranks of the working poor. They thought I'd operate on the edges of society and that my children would do the same.

I didn't want that to be me.

I was a thoughtful teen and as I thought about these things, I was determined to be one of the kids they showcased to the White people who gave money. Most people didn't care that I was in foster care and had a rough life. And since the first 15 years of my life had followed the grim statistics, how could I prove the experts wrong? How could I show my younger brother and sister that we could make it if we tried really hard? How could I show them that we could do and be anything we wanted to do and be in life?

This is what I thought about, being inspired after learning "life skills." Life skills weren't just practical, they also meant something bigger to me because they showed me that many people thought I'd never amount to anything because I had no family and a bad upbringing. During my time at Annie Malone, I outgrew the place that had given me structure and some good experiences. The agency did its best to give me a *survivor's* toolkit. But I wanted something more. I wanted the **Thriver's Toolkit.**

During most of my life, I'd played it safe. Before Annie Malone, playing it safe in life and death situations was the opposite of what most of America teaches about how to act in a violent place. If you want to survive, you strike first and hardest. In a dangerous environment, you have to use more energy to figure out when, where, and with whom to be vulnerable. Thinking back, I took a risk by letting the kid in the alley get up instead of hitting him with that brick. It was a public show of vulnerability that I wasn't used to. The irony is that playing it safe will make you live a predictable life. For me, that predictable life was prison or death or some other dead-end situation that would control me.

I didn't want that to be me.

We have to risk something, I thought. So many of us don't take risks because we don't want to feel the pain that comes from failure. But fear of failure limits your potential by keeping you in emotional and psychological "safety zones." Playing it safe gives you a predictable life, and if you have nothing, you'll have more of the same—absolutely nothing. I had to start thinking like a normal person, a person who wasn't always on edge and always angry. And I had to take a smart risk.

Taking smart risks gives you energy and creates momentum that stretches you even more, one risk at a time as you go after your goals. Taking smart risks is about believing in yourself, the quality of how you do things, and, whether you fail or succeed, how fast you bounce back or build on success. To bounce back is to get up quickly and try again. To build on success is to take the win, build on that effort, and achieve even more. It's like compound interest.

As kids, normal development means taking small steps like crawling, pulling up, and finally walking, which lead to bigger rewards and independence. Those small steps create muscle memory and positive reinforcement if you're in a healthy environment. In a broken environment, you learn to take fight-or-flight risks. Fear prompted the first big, smart risk that I remember when I told my mother that I was being sexually abused. I was five years old and feared my "uncle" would kill me and harm my siblings like he said he would. I had nightmares about what happened to me and what would happen to my family. My imagination took me to horrible places and forced a fight or flight response. I chose to fight. Now, I needed to choose to fight again.

During my sophomore year, I realized that I didn't have a Plan B. I had no backup plan. No parents, no permanent support. I learned that I would age out of care when I turned 18, and I needed a plan.

To flourish means to thrive. It means to be fulfilled and have a sense of purpose. It would be a while before achievement and flourishing were on my radar. It would be a while before I realized that I needed other people to achieve my goals, feed my hunger, and help me connect to opportunities—but I did get there.

Eventually, I realized that I couldn't keep being aggressive all the time if I wanted to have friends and be part of a community. I had to start controlling my emotions. This is critical if you want to have a community where people help each other and a future where everyone can succeed.

Unhealthy Relationships

You might stay connected in relationships you've outgrown because they feel familiar, even if they're unhealthy. My relationship with my mother should have been more than familiar; it should have been like a promise that lasted forever. Now I know that only a few relationships work for a lifetime. You have to cut out the bad relationships to build good ones with the right people who deserve your trust, time, and attention. And you must do that right now. Starting today.

Though I'm not close to many people, I've learned about functional relationships, which are relationships that work for both of you. My wife and kids give me purpose, and I give them love and security. My work relationships help me achieve more than I can alone, and I help my workmates reach their potential and share success. The people who mentor me offer advice and access, while I bring curiosity, a teachable spirit, and desire to succeed. I'm a bridge, and I pass on what I learn and give credit to the person who taught me. None of us succeed alone.

You also have to know when you've exhausted the purpose of the relationship. It usually happens when you stop growing. Knowing when to leave a relationship is as important as entering one. You don't have to be dramatic about ending relationships. When you stop showing up, it's a sign that you're cutting ties. View it as shifting your energy toward better relationships. And just because you cut ties with that person, it doesn't mean that relationship will never matter again.

Functional relationships, even true friendships that give you emotional security, are rare. When you look at your relationships, you'll get clear about who helps you achieve your goals and who doesn't.

I like to assign purposes to relationships, and then I think about what we both give and receive. That helps me decide if the relationship is balanced over time. If someone's always taking from you, that relationship isn't healthy for either of you. You don't have to stay emotionally connected to unhealthy relationships, even with family members. Unhealthy relationships inhibit your growth. When you focus on having a few high-impact relationships, you can prioritize your time and be more focused.

For example, I knew that eventually, I'd need to stop taking orders and start taking care of myself. I needed to take more control of my life. I needed more freedom. I only had a little time before I'd officially be on my own, so I got to work. I grew up and planned to build new relationships so I could make my mark on the world like Annie Malone, the entrepreneur and business leader; like my neighborhood that was once home to Black excellence; like those corporate board members and volunteers who invested so much of their time to make sure my basic needs were met.

I needed a different environment and didn't want to wait to get into the Independent Living Program. I was now seventeen and motivated to move on and chase my excellence. So, I did. I moved on and was inspired to make my mark, knowing that God had a plan for my life. The darkness of my childhood was finally giving way to a lighted path.

Tools You Can Use:

Anger can be loud, but growth is quiet. Learning to manage your emotions doesn't make you weak, it makes you powerful.

1. **Pause before reacting.** When something makes you upset, take a breath before you respond. That small pause changes everything.
2. **Find healthy outlets.** Sports, art, writing, or talking to someone can help you release what's inside instead of holding it in.
3. **See challenges as practice.** Every hard moment is a chance to practice patience, strength, and self-control.

Daily Thought: Power isn't about how much noise you make. It's about how much peace you can create.

Principles 10, 11, and 17 from *The Thriver's Toolkit* tell you to:

- Face and overcome your fears.
- Find and value mentors who help you grow.
- Develop strong leadership skills that inspire others.

CHAPTER 5
BIG CHANGES

"When I dare to be powerful, to use my strength in the service of my vision, then it becomes less and less important whether I am afraid."
—Audre Lorde

"I'm livin' my best life, ain't goin' back and forth with you."
—Lil Duval feat. Snoop Dogg, "Smile (Living My Best Life)"

In the middle of my sophomore year, I moved from the Annie Malone Children's Home to the Emergency Children's Home (ECHO). It was the perfect next step in my life. I thought, *Freedom at last!*

I remember when my case worker told me I'd be moving.

"Hello, Orvin," she said.

"Yes," I replied. I already knew why she was calling, and I felt excited. ECHO promised a place with more freedom and gave me hope that I might have a normal teenage life.

"You've been accepted," she said. I can't explain what I felt. Those words, 'You have been accepted' stayed in my mind for a long time.

I was accepted! I thought.

In ECHO's Independent Living Program, each house had between four and eight people living there. It was a busy and ever-changing environment. Unlike me, most of the other residents had moved from ECHO's residential program. The house we were in was modest and reminded me of the one I shared with Shirley. It was a humble house with two rooms upstairs, each with four beds. It held the potential for a new beginning.

ECHO had a house parent, Mr. Gerald. He was an older man with keloids on his face like Shirley. His job was to keep track of us and all the activity in the home. Mr. Gerald drove an old, beat-up red station wagon that we used to shop for food for the house.

My younger brother was also at ECHO when I got there. I'd see him around sometimes, mostly in the gym. He had friends who I thought were kind of tough, and some of them didn't live past their twenties.

The kitchen and living room at ECHO were on the first floor, which is where we had group therapy. The dorms for girls and boys in the residential side and the offices were on the other side of the campus. We had an outdoor basketball court and an indoor gym. I spent a lot of time on that court trying to get better, but I never did.

Mr. Pratt, an old White guy, was in charge of ECHO. He was the CEO. There was also Mr. Calhoun, who always had a nicely cut mini-afro and wore a suit. He was also an executive. I think he was in charge operations and was Mr. Pratt's second in command. He was older but not as old as Mr. Pratt. Mr. Calhoun was tall. *Surely*, I thought, *he played some basketball in his day.*

Mr. Calhoun would always say, "How are you today, young man?" in a firm but sincere way when we saw each other. He was like a father figure on campus.

I lived in a house with other young men. We bought groceries, cooked, and did other chores to keep the house working. Most everyone had jobs outside. We were out of the house most weekdays and came home to eat, do chores, and go to sleep. I did my homework right after school, during breaks at work, or on the bus going back to ECHO.

They were strict about the rules at ECHO. If I was going to miss curfew, I had to call, but I never missed curfew. I was driven by my desire to fit in and meet what the authority figures expected. I thought my survival depended on staying in control, which meant I often had to say "no" to myself. I blamed myself for any problems I'd had in life, and I felt I needed to "be good." My survival was also linked to being able to punish myself. Sometimes my punishment was as simple as not letting myself hang out with other kids. I didn't usually go toward fun.

Girlfriends

I liked girls, but I avoided being with them because the church and the adults in my life didn't think it was acceptable. Plus, the likely outcome of being with a girl—pregnancy and becoming a father—wasn't possible for me. I had nothing to offer.

I met Sabrina during my junior year when I was eighteen years old. She was a freshman and was fifteen years old. We both went to Gateway Tech, and I first noticed her after school when I took the same bus to work as she rode home. I was always self-conscious about being the oldest person in my class. I had a December birthday, which meant that I started school later than some, and, of course, I was older because I repeated second grade.

Sabrina had three sisters and a mom. They lived in a two-family apartment, not far from where I worked at the Schnucks Market. I fell hard for her. It wasn't like that early feeling I had with Angel, one of the first girls I ever noticed. This was different. Sabrina was smart, funny, quiet, shy, and beautiful. She was as bright as sunshine, and she had amazing hazel eyes and a strong spirit of determination. She ignited something inside me.

Sabrina and I dated for about a year. We spent a lot of time together, sharing many firsts, seconds, and thirds. I often told her that I loved her and could see us together in the future. On Saturdays, I got off work at four or five after an eight-hour shift, where I thought about her every moment—you know, real love. After that, I'd go to Sabrina's place and stayed until nine or ten. We talked about life, took walks, napped, and did whatever. When it was time to take the last bus back to ECHO, I never wanted to leave.

I cared deeply for her, so much so that I had to pull back from her during my senior year. I was afraid of getting too wrapped up in the relationship and possibly losing sight of my goal: college. Sadly, the timing of our relationship worked against us. I didn't know how to handle such intense emotions, and the easiest way out was for me to withdraw. And that opened the door for other guys to step in. I wasn't happy with the idiot she ended up with after me. She got married quickly, but I didn't have a say in her life anymore.

After Sabrina, I became a serial dater. I promised myself not to date anyone longer than six months, so I wouldn't "catch feelings." One girl I dated teased me and said I was afraid of, well, you know—sex. She said that out loud at school in front of our friends.

She said, "Orvin had a chance to get some this weekend, but he didn't take it."

I was so embarrassed, but she got a kick out of it, poking me and laughing while others hung on to her every word. I think she was trying to fit in because the cool kids were all supposedly "doing it." I wasn't sure that she'd ever done it, but she was right. She'd made moves, and maybe I had a chance with her. It wasn't that I was afraid. I just didn't want to disappoint her parents, who'd been so kind to this sewer kid.

Her dad had asked me directly, "Are you and Stephanie having sex?"

"No, sir," I said.

I was determined to keep it that way because I'd grown to respect her mom and dad. They were good people. I spent a lot of time with Stephanie and her parents and was so impressed with their two-parent family. They lived near me in one of the newly built townhomes that had a gate all around them. I used to pass by this place but never went in because of the huge gate. *I know rich people live there*, I thought. I knew they had to be rich, or at least middle class, because this was one of the first new developments I'd seen in all my years of living in the city.

Mr. Kindle, Stephanie's dad, also started asking me about college. I didn't know for sure if I wanted to go, but the seed for college had been planted. He and his wife were really interested in my future. They always asked me about my plans when I spent time with Stephanie and talked to them about life.

Stephanie knew that her next step was college. Where she was raised, it was expected. Her family lived well and treated me kindly. They were good people.

I often lay on their yellow print couch next to Stephanie. She was part girlfriend, part counselor and always wondering what was going on with me. She was fun and understood my mood. When I got quiet, she'd ask, "What's wrong, Orvin?" I often heard this same question from adults.

"Nothing," I'd say.

People always thought there was more going on with me than I showed, and they were right. I was trying to overcome an inner fight. I was trying to find faith in my abilities around people who seemed sure of themselves. I wanted to be sure of who I was as a growing boy. Besides lacking confidence in my ability to achieve great things, I struggled with how I looked. I often put myself down.

You're not handsome, I'd remind myself, and I rarely found relief from these sad thoughts.

But Stephanie would tell me I was handsome. She'd write notes, "To my handsome, good-looking friend, who I hope to soon become more than friends."

I always struggled with what to do with this. Stephanie, of course, was a beautiful girl inside and out. *Why does she think I'm handsome?* I thought.

Sabrina was my first high school sweetheart, and although I cared deeply for her, she wasn't the one to spend my life with. We were too early, too young. I didn't want us to become a distraction for each other by connecting so deeply so early in our lives.

A future with Stephanie was also unlikely for the same reason and more. It was too early, and given her middle-class background and the culturally rich and diverse environment, she was destined to succeed. She was what friends would say was "out of my league." And I needed more than to just be in love.

I was still afraid of making mistakes, so I limited myself to what felt safe. Neither Stephanie nor Sabrina felt safe because I could've easily lost myself and forgotten my goal to go to college. I was afraid of declaring my love as a teenager and committing to one person. Some high school couples did that, but it scared me. I had low self-esteem, and I overcompensated with a strong work ethic.

Friends

Lamar was my best friend from the Academy of Math and Science, and he was with me through most of my high school relationships. During this time, I got more into my writing, became closer to the Church, and started to explore part of my identity that the Church didn't seem to understand, like being a Black male.

When I wasn't playing basketball or working, I was at Lamar's house writing rap songs. Music helped me figure out who I was. I'd always liked to write. Since rap was popular, I turned my thoughts into rhymes and performed in talent shows around North St. Louis. Most of my friends were from school, ECHO, or foster care.

Lamar lived with his grandmother up the street from ECHO. Since he lived close to my group home, we became best friends. We both played basketball, cared about social issues, and loved being silly with each other. We'd hang out after school or on weekends.

Lamar would often say, "I will slap the crap out of you."

I'd say back, "I dare you." Then he'd slap me and run away while I chased him. We'd both be laughing. We loved daring each other to see who could be more crazy. It was all just fun. I trusted Lamar, and we started a rap group called Young Black Intelligence (YBI).

We were kids whose lives could have gone wrong, but we found better ways to use our time. We hung out, wrote, and practiced in Lamar's grandmother's basement. Another older guy in the neighborhood had a recording studio in his basement. The walls had foam to control sound. Lamar, his cousin E-Money, and I recorded several songs there.

YBI was important because back then, there were lots of bad images about Black boys and men on TV, in music, and everywhere. Those bad images didn't show who we really were. YBI made uplifting music. One of our first songs, "Caged Bird," was about how we sometimes felt trapped in our community.

After I moved out of ECHO, my friendship with Lamar fell apart. I don't talk to any of my childhood friends anymore. In fact, I've been disconnected from my past since high school. Most of my childhood memories are hard, so these friendships remind me of that pain and what I didn't have. Plus, life takes people different directions and that can make you lose touch.

My life had been one bad thing after another. I never learned how to handle problems like most kids do. In normal families, when kids mess up, their parents help them learn and make better choices. I never had that. Like Annie Malone, I had no family money or even parents. I had to watch people around me and learn from them.

There was a guy who used to live at ECHO but now went to Lincoln University, a Black college in Jefferson City, Missouri. He came back during school breaks in a big black car with fancy rims. I thought that was so cool. He stayed at ECHO when he was in town because he didn't have parents or other family to live with. The more I saw him, the more I could see myself as a college student.

Senior Year

At the end of my junior year, a woman named Joyce took me in. She was the woman who'd let my older brother live with her. Now I had a chance to live in a regular house in the community. I was beyond thrilled.

Joyce was a single mom who worked at the post office. No matter how she felt, she got up every day and went to work. She didn't ask much of me except to clean up after myself and do well in school. That year, she let me take the driver's test in her car, and I got my license. Having a driver's license meant I had new freedom. On most Friday nights, she let me borrow her car to go on a date or to pick up a friend and bring her back to the house to hang out. Joyce was really laid back and fun. She'd always say, "Boys will be boys."

Her adult son Deontre and nephew Steve, who also happened to be my godfather, lived with her for a while, and they really influenced me. I learned how to be more confident around girls by watching Steve, and I smoked my first joint with these guys. When my oldest brother Antwon found out, he was really upset.

He shouted, "What the heck are you doing?" as he watched me take a puff of the joint and pass it on.

Deontre was the most thoughtful Black man I knew then. He had long dreadlocks and smoked weed all the time. He liked to talk deeply about everything. He taught me about different beliefs. I didn't understand it all, but I understood that Deontre was proud to be Black. He wanted to help Black people.

I also reconnected with Djaun, a guy who'd worked at Annie Malone Children's Home but was now a director at the YMCA. One night after basketball at the Y, he asked me a question.

"Do you want to join a march to take back our streets from gang members and drug dealers?" he asked.

I said, "Sure."

We met at a mosque for a few Saturday nights. We marched the streets and chanted together and promised to take our streets back. Our group was called the Fruit of Islam. They're the security team of the Nation of Islam.

Deontre had shown me a little about Islam. But I wasn't really taught the beliefs, and I wanted to learn more. So, I bought a book called *A Message to the Black Man* by Elijah Muhammad, and I studied it.

That book and the marching taught me something important: my life as a Black man had value and purpose. I had a right to control my own life. In my senior picture, I wore denim jeans, a Tommy Hilfiger shirt, and Timberland boots. I held the book *A Message to the Black Man*. This was my message to the world. The world couldn't stand that I existed, but I wanted to be proud of being Black too. My thinking was changing.

Living with Joyce during senior year was like a dream, but I knew it wouldn't last forever. I looked at my options for after I aged out of foster care. Any direction would be hard. My first choice would be to get a job. But I'd seen lots of people who just got jobs. They lived for their paycheck. Years later, they still only had a job. I liked having money, but that wasn't for me. Joining the military was another option. I'd been in Air Force ROTC at Gateway Tech, but my whole life had been tightly controlled, and I didn't want anyone else to control me anymore. College was the final option. Even with my limited experience, I knew that education opened doors, and that's what I wanted.

I worked hard my last year and a half of high school to improve my grades. I found out that my earlier grades counted a lot toward my grade-point average, but I stayed focused anyway. I decided to apply to only one school, The University of Missouri-Columbia.

Getting Ready for College

Getting into college would be hard for me because of my low grades and lack of money. I was a below-average student, not really college material. I got a 15 on my ACT test, and every intelligence test I'd ever taken said the same thing: I was below average in math and critical thinking. Even worse, some of my social workers didn't think I could succeed. To them, I was just another kid. A kid with a welfare mom. A ward of the state. A loner with no good role models.

I'd hardly ever seen anyone from my situation make it out and do well. Sometimes I wondered if I could make it either. But I had an inner drive. I could sell my vision. When I finally got the courage, I went to Mr. Calhoun and Mrs. Reeves, the new head of ECHO. I shared my vision with them and realized that it was the first time I'd ever seen two Black leaders running an organization.

"College is my only option," I said. I didn't know exactly what that meant, but I knew what it felt like. "I want to help people like me," I added.

"We believe you can do it," they said. I begged the University of Missouri-Columbia (Mizzou) to let me in, but they didn't like my test scores and my average grades.

"Perhaps you're better suited for community college," they suggested.

I thought community college was fine for some kids. But it was like going to high school to me. I knew if I stayed in St. Louis, there were too many traps, and I could easily get caught. The old neighborhood. Old friends who weren't doing anything new. Old girls who were probably doing everyone old and new. I just couldn't risk it. I knew deep down that I needed a different environment. I needed to be somewhere that would expose me to new thoughts, thoughts that would stretch me. So, I kept trying. I didn't accept no for an answer from Mizzou.

I badgered the university for weeks, and they finally told me about a program for below-average students like me. I'd have to take a college-level math and English course during the summer at the University of Missouri-St. Louis (UMSL). If I got a grade of B or better, they'd let me in to the university. But even then, I'd be on academic probation.

The next problem was money. I needed $600 for the classes, and I didn't have it. Joyce certainly didn't have it either. I didn't even ask her. I thought, *She's being generous enough just letting me stay in her home and making sure I eat.*

After a couple of weeks, Mr. Calhoun and Mrs. Reeves called me into the office. They had news.

"We found a sponsor who will pay the $600 for you to take the classes this summer," they said.

I was thrilled. This was my last barrier. Well, except figuring out how to get to campus every day during summer. As I walked away from ECHO that day, I thought, *OK, this is real. Now, don't mess it up. You have to focus.*

I visited the UMSL campus to prepare. It was exciting and unlike any other place I'd been. It was filled with possibilities. I got a bus pass and took it to class daily. I got there as early as possible to take in the campus and study. Sometimes after class, I went to nearby Washington University to study. I'd been exposed to that campus through my high school German class, and studying there made me feel smarter.

But college was a different world. Both classes, Math and English, seemed harder than I was used to in high school. English came more naturally to me than College Algebra, so I sat up front and tried to stay focused. Algebra was like a foreign language. I just didn't get it. It was so abstract. Numbers were represented by symbols.

I don't know why this crap has to be this difficult, I thought. English class was pretty straightforward. Do this research. Write this paper. Take a position in the paper. Watch your grammar and sentence structure. You know, normal stuff. I didn't know then that numbers also tell stories.

As summer went on, I started to panic. What was I going to do about this algebra class? I talked to an advisor, and he encouraged me to talk to the instructor. But the instructor wasn't very encouraging.

"Perhaps you should consider community college," he said.

Boy, I thought, *the road to achieving anything is hard*. I wasn't having it. I didn't want to go to community college. I'd set my mind on Mizzou. Now I needed to figure out how to get there. During one discussion, our instructor said something important.

"Exceptional students chose early in the summer to test out of the math class."

That's it! I thought.

My class had students who simply didn't try hard in high school, and they were in the same boat as I was. I was a bad traditional learner. I had an IQ of 70 and 100 was average. I had a weak foundation for math. After asking more questions, I learned that *anybody* could take the exam to test out of algebra at any point. In fact, I could take it up to the final class.

I decided that the only way I could succeed was by testing out of the course. There were no limits on how many times I could take the exam, so I pumped myself up and developed a strategy I believed could help me win. It was the strategy by memory.

I'd always been able to remember lots of rap songs, songs I'd written and performed. I'd remembered the pattern of Shirley's hands on the keypad to turn off the alarm. I'd remembered all the words of defeat I'd heard. I'd remembered all the abuse. Strategy by memory was my only shot. I needed to memorize all the questions on the test and practice them. This would help me ultimately pass so I could go to the University of Missouri-Columbia.

This is life or death, I thought.

After taking the test the third time, I realized that there were different versions of the test. I took the test six times, and after each one, I wrote down everything I could remember as soon as I left the room. I would literally rush out of the room. I'd say "Thank you" as I handed my sheet in, then move quickly out the glass door to sit on the ledge. I frantically wrote down everything I could remember from the test. From those notes, I put together a practical study guide and reconstructed the equations I'd be asked to solve. As I studied my notes, I started to notice patterns and relationships. I did my best to memorize the facts of these patterns and relationships, and I practiced over and over. On the sixth time, I handed in my test, and I believed I'd nailed it.

And I did! I passed! I was going to college. Passing that math class was important, but the more important thing was what I learned about myself.

Several times during my career, potential employers have given me tests to understand my abilities. And they always say the same thing: I'm below average in math skills but outstanding in my ability to achieve. I believe that achievement comes through pushing yourself harder than the next person. Being smart doesn't equal success. I knew a lot of smart people in high school, but they often ended up being the people who just got jobs.

Achievement comes from hard work. Even today when I'm giving a speech, I make myself sit down and memorize it like I memorized those math tests. My love of language and experience rapping helped, and being aware of pitch and rhythm is the key to memorization. But in the end, you need more than tricks like that to succeed. You need discipline, focus, and persistence.

My decision to go to college also helped me understand the connection between courage and vulnerability. It took courage to say, "I'm going to college," but the vulnerability was, "I might fail." To succeed, you have to give yourself a pep talk. You have to say, "I'm going to do it scared. I'm going to do it anyway."

Imagine if Annie Malone had given up. Imagine if she'd listened to the people who told her, "You can't succeed! You're a woman. You're Black. You don't have a family background." There would've been no Poro Beauty Products. No Poro College. No Annie Malone Children's Home. Instead, she had a vision and made it a reality.

Tools You Can Use:

Change can feel scary, but it's also a sign that you're growing. Every time you step into something new, you're proving you can adapt.

1. **Be open to new beginnings.** Change might mean leaving something behind, but it also means stepping toward something better.
2. **Work through the uncomfortable.** Growth never feels easy at first—that's how you know it's working.
3. **Keep your values close.** Even as things around you shift, hold tight to who you are and what matters most.

Daily Thought: You can't control change, but you can control how you show up for it.

Principles 6, 9, and 12 from *The Thriver's Toolkit* tell you to:

- Accept change and see it as a way to grow.
- Know your worth and see yourself as valuable.
- Work hard and stay dedicated to what matters most.

CHAPTER 6
COLLEGE LIFE

"When you have mastered numbers, you will in fact no longer be reading numbers, any more than you read words when reading books. You will be reading meanings."

—*W.E.B. DuBois*

"It's beauty in the struggle, ugliness in the success."

—*J. Cole, "Love Yourz"*

It was hard to process that I'd gotten into college. But I had a vision and kept moving toward it.

"How does it feel?" I was asked.

"It feels great. I'm so proud," I'd say.

And that was true. I did feel great. I was proud that I'd set my mind to a very hard task and had accomplished it. But I also felt like a fake. I was afraid. Actually, I was terrified. I had so many unanswered questions in my mind. *What if I didn't have more to give?* I thought. *What if testing out of a class that I was failing was my last move?* I wondered. *What if I can't outsmart the system? Or even more, what if I'm just not good enough to complete college-level work?*

I would have no more convenient explanations about why I was behind in life. No more excuses like poverty, a bad education, the death of my mom, an absent dad, abuse, and foster care. I'd earned a chance that many didn't get. And I believed there was a high probability that I would mess up that chance. It was a heavy burden I carried.

Mizzou heavily recruited Black students in 1994, and they offered a full-ride African American scholarship. Still struggling to become racially diverse, the largest group of Black students in Mizzou's history was recruited. About 600 strong were recruited to a campus population of around 20,000.

Many of my friends went to other colleges. My good friend Hubert, with whom I played basketball and hung out socially, was bound for St. Louis University (SLU). SLU was a tough school to get into, and Hubert was pretty good in math, I remembered. The year before, Janine went to Purdue University in Lafayette, Indiana. She was a good friend and daughter of my junior varsity basketball coach. I thought it must be something to have the confidence to go all the way to Indiana.

"Purdue is only four hours away," she said. But that seemed like a whole world away to me.

Lamar decided to attend the historically Black college, Lane College, in Jackson, Tennessee. Even with all my Black consciousness, I didn't know much about Historically Black Colleges and Universities (HBCUs). That's when I learned that Black and White schools had official designations. An HBCU is any historically Black college or university that was started before 1964. Its main job was, and still is, to educate Black Americans. It also has to be approved by a nationally recognized group that checks colleges.

A Predominantly White Institution (PWI) is a university that has 50% or more enrolled White students. It's also used to refer to any university that's deemed "historically White."

Where I lived had changed so many times throughout childhood and high school. This always meant big change. I started life in East St. Louis. Then moved to North St. Louis where mom died. Then I moved in with Shirley before she had her stroke. Then was sent to Annie Malone, and I lived in orphanages until I moved in with Joyce. But the most dramatic change was moving to the University of Missouri-Columbia for college.

It was the first time I'd been out of the city of St. Louis since I was nine. I'd never seen the acres of farmland, small towns, or middle-of-nowhere gas stations that dotted the 90-minute drive to Columbia. When I got to town, the campus was alive with activity. Young adults were all over the place. They were joking around and laughing as they unloaded their parents' cars and U-Hauls packed full of clothes, TVs, stereos, food, everything.

Mizzou was the whitest place I'd ever seen. *This is definitely a PWI,* I thought as I took it all in. It was intimidating, to say the least. White people, who seemingly had it all, were everywhere. I had to battle my thoughts even more in their presence. In my world, I'd been wrongly taught that they were the best example of success.

My belongings were miniscule compared to theirs. I felt alone, so I called Shirley's sister, Brenda. She was the only person I knew in town. I'd always looked up to Brenda and her husband, Charles. They seemed like they had it all together. It wasn't their fault that Shirley preferred their kids, Deanna and Russ, over us. Brenda always had positive energy, and when she pulled up, I could see her big smile and the gap in her teeth as I stepped out of the dorm.

She reached over the seat as I entered. She hugged me, showing pride, stating, "I'm so glad to see you."

I settled into the car with mixed emotions. I was definitely excited to see her. But I was also in a dark mood because I hadn't gotten to see her more often when I was growing up. As we made our way to Walmart, I wondered what my life would've been like if she'd been the one to raise the four of us instead of Shirley.

I didn't know what to expect on this shopping trip. I wondered if we would pick out things, and while standing at the checkout register, Brenda would disappear. Instead, she loaded my cart with snacks and supplies. She didn't disappear but, instead, whipped out her credit card to cover the bill. I couldn't help but look at her with gratitude. It was one of the nicest things anyone had ever done for me. Afterward, she dropped me off, and I made several trips from the car to my dorm room. I hugged Brenda once more as I got the last load. I thought, *This was a very good day filled with kindness.*

Over the weekend, I settled into my dorm and explored the campus. One evening, I heard some guys outside who rapped and laughed. I thought, *Rappers at Mizzou—no way!* I went downstairs and out the door to meet a group that included J-Scott.

Years later, we pledged the same fraternity, Alpha Phi Alpha. After high school, I promised that if I was going to be successful in college, I needed to focus. I couldn't commit the time that I'd once put into music. So, despite how excited I felt when I saw rappers on campus, I pulled away from that group as quickly as I had joined.

I walked the campus and watched the White Greek row near my dorm and across the street from the tracks at Rothwell Gym. White Greeks partied hard that weekend and most every week-end. I connected with freshmen on a basketball court late at night. We played ball. This was cool because it reminded me a bit of the outdoor court at the Annie Malone Children's Home and ECHO. It helped me get used to my new environment.

Money Issues

After I checked into my dorm, my first official visit was with the financial aid office in Jesse Hall, Mizzou's main office building. It was a big, red-brick building. I could see its white dome from a distance. I was in good spirits and had really sunk into my thoughts about life as I walked. I felt good about the meeting. I looked at the signs for directions to the financial aid office on the lower level.

As I entered the basement, I was welcomed by what looked like a dungeon. It was a dimly lit space with an institutional feel that could've cast a shadow on what was supposed to be a joyous moment. But I felt nothing but joy as I waited my turn. I looked forward to hearing how much extra money I'd get in scholarships that I could apply to my other expenses. *Certainly*, I thought, *I can buy a car with the money left over after I pay for the dorm, classes, books, and other expenses like the gym and health care.* Every Black student I'd known at Mizzou told me they'd gotten the scholarship, so I thought it was a sure thing. After all, I was Black, too.

"Orvin Kimbrough," the financial aid person called out.

"Yes, that's me," I said enthusiastically.

After I made my way into his office, sat down, and exchanged small talk while he got information about me, he delivered the shocking news. What was supposed to be a good moment turned dark.

"Oh, you don't qualify for any scholarships."

"That can't be," I insisted.

"No, Orvin, I'm certain about this. Students who are on academic probation aren't eligible for scholarships," he said. I wondered why they didn't tell me that before I got to campus. It would've saved me a trip to Columbia. Now, how would I get back to St. Louis?

I had worked so hard to get to this point. My mind was racing. I sunk into a whirlwind of negative thoughts and felt my mood shift. *The deck is always stacked against me,* I thought. It's two steps forward, three steps backward.

"But you do qualify for loans," he said.

I perked up. I'd just heard the word "qualify."

"I qualify for what?" I said.

He said something about a Pell grant and something else about it being backed by the government. He may as well have been speaking a foreign language because I had no idea what he was talking about. But his tone seemed to say that I could stay at Mizzou if I did what he asked of me.

"You need to fill out some paperwork to see how much you qualify for," he said. "Given your circumstance as a ward of the State, you should be eligible for the maximum amount. This will more than cover your tuition, dorm, and other college expenses," he said.

His words gave me a lifeline. I held on to the thin hope that he was correct. *I can't go back home,* I thought.

He gave me the paperwork, and we worked through the documents together. It was simple because I didn't have any income and no parents. This was my first loan, and I didn't know what I was doing. But by filling out that paperwork, I was making some kind of investment in myself. An investment in my future.

And bingo! He was correct. I qualified for the maximum loan amount, so that's what I asked for. The maximum amount. It was like hitting the jackpot. They gave me provisional approval, and I went back sometime later to pick up the surplus. And the amount exceeded what I needed for direct educational expenses. I was overjoyed. The fall of 1994 was a defining moment as my college adventure began.

I walked out of the building feeling hopeful and ready to start my college life. I continued to explore the campus further and set out on a journey to find out where my classes were. Jesse Hall was great, and the rest of campus was equally stunning. I'd only known St. Louis City, with its streets on a grid, many run-down houses, and danger around every corner. The campus was like a park. Full of grass and trees with beautiful buildings spread out all over it.

I soon learned that there were actually two campuses. The older "red campus," where Jesse Hall was, felt more comfortable to me because the buildings were made of red brick. Just like the buildings at home. Those buildings surrounded a central green space, Francis Quadrangle, and the famous Columns stood in the center of the quadrangle. They reminded me of those big columns in front of the Annie Malone Children's Home, but they didn't hold up a roof. They were all that was left after the university's academic hall burned to the ground in 1892.

The other campus was the "white campus," where the buildings were made of limestone. In the coming years, I'd spend a lot of time walking this part of campus, which was friendly and welcoming.

Students were everywhere, playing frisbee and hacky sack and talking and laughing. They all seemed so happy and full of life. It was hard for me to believe that this would be my home for the next four years, but here I was. I wanted to major in physical therapy because that was a helping profession, similar to my occupational therapy internship in high school.

I'm now a real student at the University of Missouri-Columbia, I thought. Saying the university's full name out loud gave me chills. It felt like I'd accomplished something great. There was so much respect for that name and institution in my home state of Missouri.

As I thought about those big, white columns and walked around campus that day, I thought about my life up to that point. The boy who had wanted to be Superman, who had the courage to climb up on that dresser, to the tallest point in the room and jump off, had found that courage again after years of abuse and neglect. I didn't know exactly what I wanted yet, but I did know what I did *not* want. I didn't want to stay in the cycle of poverty. I didn't want a life like some of the kids I'd grown up with, kids who joined gangs, got pregnant, and went to jail. I didn't want addiction. I didn't want any part of the life I seemed destined to live, and I was doing it. I unlocked my future, and college was the key.

I'd focused on survival for so long and felt like I constantly lived on a fault line. I just waited for the next big quake to come. The

Annie Malone Children's Home and ECHO had given me just enough space to imagine that my life could be something better. I started to overcome my fear of being like my parents and found faith that my life had value, purpose, and meaning, and maybe, just maybe, it was part of a story that was bigger than me. Still, that decision to go to college had been one of the scariest, most challenging decisions I'd ever made, and though I didn't realize it then, my college years would push me in ways I couldn't yet imagine.

Hard Classes

I'd settled into my dorm, registered for my classes, and gotten all my books. Now what? The first few months of college were a blur. I had classes on Mondays, Wednesdays, and Fridays. My nemesis, College Algebra, was back, and so was Biology and Biology lab, which I didn't like. There were so many students everywhere. This was the first time I'd ever sat in an auditorium with nearly 400 other students to learn a subject. This was mass-produced education at its best. No matter my study habits, which I developed and improved, I found myself more and more lost, and the worst part was that I didn't know how or where to get help.

There was a Laotian kid from my high school, Joey, who lived in my dorm. We connected often. He was a smart kid who majored in math. Sometimes, he'd help me with my college algebra class, but I was beyond help. This class swallowed me like a python. I felt my very airways constrict with the pressure. I fidgeted anxiously as if I expected Shirley's blow from a wrong answer. Each assignment sent me into a panic because it stood between me and success, a 2.0 GPA, which I had to achieve to stay at Mizzou.

The campus buzzed with activity. Students moved between classes. Laughter echoed through the hallways. But I preferred the quiet corners of the library. The silence was comfortable, a stark contrast to the chaotic energy outside.

Every day, I followed the same routine. Wake up, attend classes, mostly study alone in the library, and return to my dorm. Sometimes my dorm neighbor would drop by to say, "What's up Orvin?" and shoot the breeze, or someone else would invite me for a ride to Walmart or to pick up food. But these connections were brief, quick moments in an otherwise solitary and welcomed existence.

As I sat near Lowry Mall, my mind wandered. I watched groups of friends who laughed and studied together. A pang of loneliness hit me. I knew I had isolated myself, but the fear of deeper connections held me back. *It's safer this way*, I thought. *No complications, no distractions.*

I had one female friend who provided brief escapes from my isolation. We met up sometimes and enjoyed casual encounters and conversations that never went too deep. She had a long-time boyfriend back in St. Louis, and I was fine with our friends-with-benefits relationship. I didn't want anything serious. It was a perfect arrangement for me because, more than anything, I valued my solitude.

Over Christmas break, she became distant. I noticed the changes: fewer calls, shorter conversations, longer pauses. Then one day she phoned and told me she was pregnant and wouldn't be coming back for the next semester.

For a moment, I had an out-of-body experience. My mind raced: *Could this be mine?* Then I reminded myself of one thing I had done right, something I'd learned in those life-skills courses. It wasn't a guarantee, but I'd always worn protection.

She was clear that the baby wasn't mine. I heard the pain in her voice and could almost feel the tears on her face through the phone. I sat quietly. The weight of her words sank in. I thought about her, about my own journey up to that point, and how lucky I was that she didn't tell me I was going to be a father.

When she didn't come back, the campus felt even emptier.

Some days, I didn't know how I would make it. I, too, was pregnant with the fear of defeat. I didn't want to birth this idea. I hadn't yet learned about the student support services on campus, and I'm not sure that if I'd known about them, I would have felt comfortable to use them. I tried hard to develop stronger study skills. I studied a lot, but did I study the right things?

At Annie Malone, I didn't like the structure they put on me, but college demanded a different kind of structure. Annie Malone had guided my day-to-day life—when to wake up, brush my teeth, eat, and what to do with my money. But college presented a different challenge. College said, "Here's the goal, now figure out how to get there." This, I learned, is so important to achieve anything in life. But first, I had to make it through College Algebra.

The summer class had shown me how hard this would be. I couldn't take a test-out exam over and over again. Now, I encountered numerical expressions, theories, and abstract ideas that floated in the air, detached from reality. To add to the challenge, the class was massive, with hundreds of young adults crammed into an auditorium. They struggled with the content in what they called a "weed-out course."

What does that mean? I wondered. It soon became clear that this course was designed to sift through the masses and determine who was college material and who wasn't. I feared I'd be deemed unsuitable for college if this course was the judge. I was scared to ask questions in front of such a huge group or admit I needed extra time. Despite my best efforts, my fear of academic probation grew stronger on test days and weighed me down with intense anxiety.

I had one clear goal: to achieve a 2.0 GPA. This became my daily mantra, "2.0." I focused on that every day. I was careful about my studies and did the very best I could. As the semester ended and I took my last College Algebra and Biology test, I felt I was hanging on by a thread. I wouldn't get my final grades right away; they mailed them out over Christmas break.

Flunked Out

I hitched a ride back to St. Louis and waited for my grades while I stayed with Joyce. Soon enough, I learned that I'd earned a C in most classes, a B in a history and social studies course, and a D in College Algebra, which is what I expected. *I did it!* I thought. I was certain my B would offset the D in College Algebra because the classes were weighted the same, but not so fast. I read further and realized that not only did I earn a D in Algebra, but I also earned a D in Biology Lab, which was a two-credit hour course. The two classes combined were enough to sink my GPA to 1.8—and my stomach sank. I was in agony.

Shortly after, I received a letter in the mail with the bad news: "Orvin, you earned a 1.8 GPA, and you needed to maintain a 2.0 GPA. You are officially withdrawn from the school."

"No! This cannot happen. I flunked out of school!" I cried.

I was crushed. I immediately thought about all the people who had cheered me on—the teachers, the state workers, the folks at ECHO who celebrated me "because I was so rare." I thought about my mentors, the people from the church, community-based organizations, my godmother, and others to whom I had proudly declared that I would go to college. They were genuinely happy for me.

So many had invested in me and helped me get on a path where I could stop feeling like just another poor kid who needed to be stabilized to get through high school, only to be dumped out on the streets of North St. Louis.

"Orvin, you have real potential," they'd often said. I thought about this now more than I had when I was in good standing and in college.

I thought about the negative thoughts that wouldn't leave me alone during my effort to get into college. Those thoughts had convinced me that the challenges were too great for me to overcome, at least in the way I wanted. They said, *Your mom was an addict, your dad was absent, you don't have a chance.* Now, I was failing the people who had championed me. I was on the verge of becoming what the statistics had said I would become. Through my silent tears, I promised not to tell anybody about this, and I slipped into a depression.

After several days, I built up the courage to call the Dean of Students. I was so ashamed that I literally begged him to take me back, to give me another chance.

"If you don't give me another shot, I'm not going to make it," I said.

And I meant exactly that. Not that I would have to settle for a lower level of success, but that I literally *would not make it*. I wouldn't survive. I felt this deeply, and it was a life-or-death moment.

He said, "Make your way to Columbia so we can discuss this."

I told him that I had no transportation to Columbia and after he heard me out, he finally said, "OK, one more chance, but this is it. If you can't turn it around in the spring semester, I don't know what to tell you."

I'd thrown myself humbly at his feet and firmly stated, "I won't let you down." And I meant it.

My 1.8 GPA didn't mean I hadn't tried hard; it meant I fell a little short of the goal. By missing the 2.0 grade point average mark, it became clear that things were literally black and white. There was no gray. However, there were people in the world, like this Dean of Students, who had the power to see gray if they believed the risk was worth it. I was on the borderline of success, and I needed something that felt small to others but was gigantic to me. I needed one more chance. I needed a small gesture to break in my favor. I'd never been prepared for college, and I needed one more shot. And one person had the power to do that.

Now, I no longer let myself think that I could fail. To fail was to lose everything I wanted in life. I knew that this time, I'd have to channel my energy differently. By falling just a little short the first time around, I could see success.

I needed greater focus. I needed mental clarity. I needed to align myself with the right people who had the right mindset to win. I needed to see that I still had a chance at writing a new story.

Tools You Can Use:

Starting fresh in a new place can bring pressure, excitement, and fear all at once. But courage isn't the absence of fear—it's choosing to move anyway.

1. **Stay disciplined.** Success doesn't happen overnight. It's built by doing small things well over and over again.
2. **Ask for help early.** You don't have to know everything. Learning how to ask questions shows strength, not weakness.
3. **Be honest about what you feel.** Sometimes you just need to name it—fear, stress, excitement—to start working through it.

Daily Thought: The first step is often the hardest, but it's also the one that proves you can do it.

Principles 11, 18, and 21 from *The Thriver's Toolkit* tell you to:

- Find and value mentors who help you grow.
- Have faith in yourself and your journey.
- Be vulnerable. It builds real strength and connection.

CHAPTER 7

SERIOUS STUDENT

"I really don't think life is about the I-could-have-beens.
Life is only about the I-tried-to-do.
I don't mind the failure, but I can't imagine that
I'd forgive myself if I didn't try."
—Nikki Giovanni

"We gotta make a change.
It's time for us as a people to start makin' some changes.
Let's change the way we eat, let's change the way we live,
and let's change the way we treat each other."
—Tupac Shakur, "Changes"

I was so close to making it, which meant that to overcome poverty, I was doing something different. And my "something different" was going to college. My oldest brother had gone to college on a football scholarship. Though we never discussed his academic progress, I later learned he didn't graduate until he was an adult. I was proud when he finally completed his degree.

When I told the dean of students that "I'm not going to make it" if he didn't let me back in, the truth was that I couldn't picture my life without a college degree. I needed a college degree like I needed oxygen or water. It was tied to my survival. I was passionate about getting my college degree because, other than the money made by drug dealers, the most successful Black people I'd seen were entertainers or sports figures. There's nothing wrong with that and the success that comes those professions because these people had to lean into their God-given gifts. But I was neither athletic nor an entertainer.

I knew many successful Black people who were gifted tradesmen who made good money. I'd been exposed to trades in high school and when I worked for Mr. Weeden, the first Black business owner I knew who owned a construction company, but I wasn't particularly handy. Trade school wouldn't have suited me. My gift was my mind. I'd always been a thoughtful and serious thinker. I believed I could become a really good student and use that to get a meaningful job later that would help me rise above poverty.

Racial Differences

I was introduced to lots of different ideas and people from all kinds of backgrounds in college. I'd learned to look for the good in others and to connect with people who were often left out. That helped me understand people with different views and led to strong discussions about poverty and how society thinks about it.

In the 1990s, poverty was often discussed in terms of race. Our talks in sociology and Black studies asked a question: did poverty come from personal problems or system problems? These talks were eye-opening. I learned that the idea that "people succeed all by themselves" is wrong and that government rules and laws really change people's lives.

"Is being in poverty someone's fault?" my professor asked loudly. We all looked away or looked at the floor. We didn't want to be called on. It was always interesting to see who would speak first.

He asked the question again but added more. He made it personal.

"Is anyone's poverty their own fault? Is it because of their choices, their lack of smarts, and their lack of effort?"

He looked out at our silent, awkward faces. "Of course not," he said, "but some people believe that. It's a dangerous story. Why would we believe this?" he asked.

By this time, I knew he would answer his own question. But just then, I saw a hand shoot up. It was a young White kid with a stocky build and blond hair.

"Yes, sir," the professor said.

"My great-grandfather came to this country. He fought in the war. He used the GI bill, went to school, and started a business." He stopped and tried to find the right words. "I guess people think there are folks who've been here a long time, but we still have to support them with our tax money. They haven't done anything to help themselves."

I'd heard some version of this before. He meant that Black people had been given every chance to succeed, but we're still behind because we don't work hard.

I had to fight back emotion when I said sharply, "It's been less than thirty years since the law allowed Black people to be educated fairly. I wish my great-grandfather had an opportunity with the GI bill."

I was learning something new. Outside my poor neighborhood, people really believed Americans succeed because they work hard and do it all by themselves. They didn't think about how the government and its laws can help you or hurt you. I'd only seen government help in the form of welfare. Now I started to see there's a difference between help that lets you build something and help that makes you want to give up.

I wanted to learn more about my history, so I took as many Black history courses as possible. These were the only times I met Black professors. I read a lot and found stories about important people like Mary McLeod Bethune. Her parents had been slaves. Even with such a hard start, Bethune became a leader in education, women's rights, and civil rights. She started what's now called Bethune-Cookman College in 1929.

Benjamin Banneker's story connected with me too. His dad had been a slave, and his mom had been an indentured servant. He taught himself and became a famous surveyor, astronomer, and almanac writer. His story proved that you don't need formal education to succeed.

I was shocked to learn that the first African American to win the Nobel Peace Prize wasn't Dr. Martin Luther King Jr., but Ralph Bunche. I wondered if he was related to my high school basketball coach, Mr. Bunche.

I was fascinated by Madam C.J. Walker. Her parents had been slaves and worked as sharecroppers, so she grew up poor. She became one of the richest and most powerful women of her time. She started with just $1.25 and built a successful hair care business for African American women. She created it because she was losing her own hair.

These leaders taught me a crucial lesson about success: when you start from behind, you have to work harder, focus more, and think differently than most people. You have to keep going longer too. All of these trailblazers did exactly that. They showed what it means to beat the odds and make things easier for people who came after them.

Even during debates and intense discussions, I never lost sight of the fact that my gift was about actually seeing other people. Regardless of our disagreements, like the idea that Black people don't work hard enough, as suggested by a classmate, I didn't see that guy as a bad person. I simply thought he was misinformed. I leaned into my gift of encouragement.

Getting Ahead

The harder I tried, the better I got. I succeeded by consistently putting forth effort. I worked hard. Whenever I could get extra credit coursework to round out my grades or provide a buffer, I went after it and was totally focused.

"You got this," I would say to myself as I walked to class on test days.

Not only did I attend classes, but I also worked at JCPenney while I was in college. The managers there were all fairly encouraging. Other than my time at Schnucks, it was the first time I felt a sense of community in a large company.

"You could be a manager at Penney's after college," they said.

Wow, "after college" was a nice idea. Early in my college experience, people helped transform what they saw as my gifts into a market opportunity. Many people took me seriously, even when others didn't believe in me. These people went beyond belief and kind words to offer me help. A helping hand, like the one given by the Dean of Students is critical to success.

I thought about the young people in my neighborhood. So many of us needed to get lucky and meet just one person who took a real interest in helping us see the possibilities. This entire picture of hard work, effort, and persistence is often useless unless there's also a helping hand. You need both, but a helping hand is crucial.

Inspiration vs. Motivation

Being *inspired* to do something versus having the internal drive or *motivation* to do something are different. Inspiration and motivation have both been key to my achievements. Inspiration is a powerful energy to act that comes from outside sources. For example, my oldest brother was a football player. It wasn't the football that inspired me but his discipline. He got up every day and put in the work.

Inspiration is a function of what you've lived. Growing up in North St. Louis with its gangs, drugs, fatherless households, and the women who carried a heavy burden but kept moving inspired me. Seeing the way the church stepped up to provide food, clothing, and spiritual assistance inspired me. The church was the last pillar of hope in our community, which was filled with payday loans and liquor stores.

Motivation, however, comes from inside you. It's the thing that gives you the will to move. Motivation and inspiration are different sides of the same coin. I was motivated to get back into college for several reasons, including the fear of the "tried but failed" sign that the world would hand me. Instead, I chose to believe that I just fell a little short of the goal, not that I was a failure. I saw other people who'd just barely made it, meaning their grades looked like mine, except they had one good break. I was motivated to do what they did and more.

Motivation comes from how you were raised, where you live, and what you think is right and fair. It's what makes you keep trying and moving forward in a world that judges you harshly and doesn't forgive mistakes. Both inspiration and motivation work together if you allow the momentum to work in and through you.

Back to School

During Christmas Break in 1994, I turned 20 years old. I was so thankful to have been given the perfect gift—one more chance by the Dean of Students. I couldn't wait to get back to Mizzou for the spring semester. This was my last shot, and I was ready to take on college as a system that wasn't designed for me. Even though I hadn't done well, it was also true that the university wasn't ready for Black students. They especially weren't ready for poor students like me who'd grown up without good schools or money or even parents.

I started to think about life as one big chess game. I knew the system was set up for me and anyone who grew up like me to fail, but even so, simply because I was born in America, I had it better than most people in the world. Public education, success, and failure were all I could think about during that Christmas break. I remember thinking that public education was produced the same way that cars were made.

"Education is, by and large, mass-produced; it's an assembly line," I argued passionately during late-night, deep discussions.

I thought there weren't enough resources to help people like me figure out how to learn best and create a learning experience that worked for us. I spent most of my childhood and early college thinking I was a failure and not as smart as others. It turns out I just didn't have a good foundation, and because of that, I needed different tools and support. To make this work, I needed to talk to myself differently, get organized differently, and use my energy differently. With the right support, I could use my learning style and find success.

As soon as I read the words, "Orvin, you have been dismissed from school," and gathered my composure, I knew what to tell myself. I'd had a lifetime of speaking things into being by saying them over and over until they became real. So that entire break, I said, *All right. I'm going back; I can do this. I'm an exceptional learner. I just learn differently, and I'm going to figure this out.*

Since I was playing a game of strategy, I first had to figure out the rules. I'd been so excited to get into college that I'd never understood the rules of engagement. I took fifteen credit hours that first semester because I thought I had to. With College Algebra looming, I had to find more time to study because it would need my undivided attention. *How can I give this three-credit hour course my undivided attention if I take five courses?* I couldn't. So, before I went back to campus, I phoned my advisor for advice.

"Do I have to take 15 credit hours to stay in school?" I asked.

"Oh no," she said. "Twelve credit hours is all that's required for you to maintain full-time status and keep your government-backed loans."

So, I cut my schedule back to twelve hours and then complemented College Algebra with other elective courses that I enjoyed, like history and social work. *The blessing,* I thought, *is this time, I can take the course in a smaller class setting.* This was a huge win. I also enrolled in math tutoring every day after the lecture.

I also took an introductory social work class where I met Dr. Janice Chadda. Because of her interest in me, I changed my major and my life. I'd been disconnected from people and the world around me, and I thought most people had low expectations of me, due to the challenges of my youth. And, because the news highlighted crime and violence in urban areas way too much. That created a stereotype that Black boys were either criminals or victims of crime. It even made negative stereotypes stronger and reinforced biased views. Black boys were connected with drug-related activities and the stereotype of Black males as criminals and troublemakers increased.

I often shared with younger poor kids, my siblings included, that to most of America and the world, Black kids were throwaways. That meant *we* were throwaways. If you watched how people like me were depicted by politicians and others in power, you'd learn that we had no worth or work ethic. We had no value for life and no values in life. We weren't worth the welfare that only some of us received, but all were suspected to receive.

The Challenges Ahead

As I entered my second semester, I was unsure about my family and my place in the world. But I was determined to put forth my best effort to change the story of my life. I was proud that I'd made it back. I was also obsessed with how much time I had to live to do what God had placed in my heart.

Both fear and faith motivated me. The deaths of Shirley and my mom were a fear that pushed me hard. I didn't think I had time on my side. Shirley had recently passed away, and my mother had died at just 28 years old. I thought that might be my fate too.

But faith told me something different. It reminded me that if I focused on what I could control and invited the right people into my life, I could still move forward. So, I turned inward and became even more determined. My challenges were big, really big, but a few things helped me.

After spending my first semester mostly alone, I started meeting kind people who encouraged me. I also began applying what I was learning in my social work classes, especially a powerful idea called the strengths perspective.

A strengths perspective means focusing on your abilities, talents, skills, and dreams instead of your weaknesses or everything that's gone wrong. It's about seeing possibilities instead of limits. That shift, which Dr. Chaddha, my Introductory Social Work professor, taught me, changed the way I saw myself and my life.

One day, I realized that I needed to do something with all the emotions I carried from childhood: the pain of trauma, failure, and feeling forgotten by society. I couldn't let those emotions control me anymore. I needed to take what was within my power and use it. I had to picture a new vision for my future. I couldn't depend on other people to create it for me. I had to become my own champion and channel my energy toward moving forward.

When I looked out at the world, I didn't always see hope. Sometimes, it seemed like the world hated me. That created fear, but I knew I needed faith instead. So, I began reframing the negatives and drawing energy from them.

I learned that pain could become fuel if I used it that way. That simple shift helped me gain energy not only from the positive people and things around me but also from the negative ones. My strengths perspective had come full circle.

Something else happened too. As I leaned into that strength and learned more about how my mind worked, I began to believe maybe I wasn't that "dumb, stupid kid" after all. I discovered that understanding how you learn, grow, and achieve is an important first step toward success. Once you know those things about yourself, you never stop building on them.

For many years, I hadn't cared much about school. But college changed that. When information was presented in an interesting and practical way, I realized I could learn, and I wanted to.

Outside of class, I began volunteering at the local Boys & Girls Club. I shared an important message with the young people there: "Failing in school doesn't mean you're a failure. Sometimes you struggle because of how information is presented." I always added, though, that effort matters. You have to give your best.

There will always be subjects you dislike. For me, it was College Algebra, but facing challenges is part of achieving your goals.

For the first time, I realized I loved learning and was naturally curious. I could wake up before dawn and study all day without missing my friends. I also liked studying in groups. They gave me a way to measure my progress and pushed me to do better.

I only competed against my own previous achievements. I learned that I did best when the material was connected to real life rather than being abstract. I thrived in smaller groups and needed a personalized learning plan.

So, I built a structure and system that I could repeat and apply to everything I studied, and it worked.

I often walked around campus talking to myself, asking questions like, "What's the big idea here?" and "How do I break this into smaller parts?" Once I could see how the pieces fit together, from a sentence to a paragraph, from a paragraph to a page, I began to truly learn. It didn't matter if it was history or math. I established a rhythm I could remember and built layer upon layer of knowledge on top of it.

By the end of the semester, I was confident I had achieved what I set out to do. I passed College Algebra and did well in all my courses. In May of 1995, I headed home for summer break, not just as a student who had passed his classes, but as a young man who had started to believe in himself.

After my first semester, I'd learned that I might fall short, but I couldn't consider that a complete failure. I began to see failure as a short-term glitch, just a moment when I fell short of victory. If I kept projecting a powerful vision and stayed patient and persistent, I knew I would eventually win.

On the car ride home, I didn't think about the possibility of failure. I decided to receive all that God had positioned me to take. I thought about the spring semester and realized what a huge achievement it had been. I also thought about the path I didn't take. The easiest route would have been to do what everyone else around me was doing.

That's why so many of my childhood friends ended up selling drugs, why so many became parents too young, and why so many ended up dead, in jail, or in jobs with no purpose. Keeping up with the Joneses was alive and well, but it could be a race to the bottom if that's all you know.

Where you come from and where you live are powerful forces. Even when that path conflicts with your inner compass, it's easier to go along with what's familiar.

Inspiration is important, but it doesn't always push us to act differently. When you see someone from a similar background who's faced the same challenges and achieved something great, it lights a spark. But inspiration alone isn't enough. I've seen people get inspired and then fall back into old habits once the feeling fades.

To turn inspiration into action, you need an engine, a constant source of energy. I call this an activator. And the most powerful activator, the one that bridges the gap between inspiration and motivation, is faith.

Setbacks are part of the journey, but accepting failure is not. Failure only happens when you stop trying. You have to commit to a relentless pursuit until you succeed.

This toughness, this unyielding effort, is what I chose. I began to see myself through a divine lens as more than a conqueror. That image of myself, strengthened by faith and God's grace, gave me confidence that I would overcome any challenge in my path. My journey wasn't only about earning a degree. It was proof that faith is the ultimate activator, faith that turns inspiration into real achievement.

I fully embraced the saying, "If at first you don't succeed, try, try again." And I committed my whole heart to living it.

TOOLS YOU CAN USE

When you start to take school, work, or your goals seriously, everything changes. Focus isn't about perfection, it's about purpose.

1. **Set clear goals.** Know what you're working toward and remind yourself why it matters.
2. **Protect your focus.** Don't let distractions or negativity pull you off track.
3. **Surround yourself with motivated people.** Who you hang around will shape what you believe is possible.

Daily Thought: Focus is like a muscle: the more you use it, the stronger it gets.

Principles 7, 8, and 13 from *The Thriver's Toolkit* tell you to:

- Set clear goals and plan for the future.
- Embrace lifelong learning as a way of growing stronger.
- Keep a positive attitude, even when things get tough.

CHAPTER 8
NEW OPPORTUNITIES

"If you wanna fly, you got to give up the sh*t that weighs you down."
—*Toni Morrison*

"Find your purpose or you wastin' air."
—*Nipsey Hussle, "Victory Lap"*

That summer, I lived with Joyce and worked two jobs. One job was with the Division of Family Services. I worked for Mrs. Marie Thomas, who was a leader of a program I'd been in when I lived in a group home. My other job was at Popeye's Chicken. I took public transportation to get to work every day.

My mission that summer was to save enough money to pay off a maxed-out credit card. I'd foolishly applied for it just to get a free T-shirt. The credit card people didn't care that I didn't have a job or any way to pay them back. They just handed me a credit card, and like any teenager, I thought it was free money. I maxed out the $500 limit and tried to avoid their calls. I felt terrible about it, but I was trapped. I wanted to get out of that mess. My other goal was to move off campus, and to do that, I had to buy a car so I could get back and forth to my classes.

Popeye's Chicken barely paid more than $4.25 per hour. But the other job paid between $10 and $15 per hour. The only problem was that the hours were limited. After I told Mrs. Thomas about my work situation and my money goals for the summer, she managed to more than double my hours. So, now I was working nearly full-time. I really appreciated and valued that work. And because I was making more money and spending less time, everything was more fulfilling.

New Opportunities

Mrs. Thomas was one of the kindest people I'd ever met. She was my boss, but she also encouraged me. She even got me my first paid speaking job. That's when I started to realize the power of words and writing.

One day, she asked me a question that would change my life.

"Would you like to be the main speaker at the annual State of Missouri Child Welfare Conference?"

I wasn't sure she was talking to me because she sounded so casual. She also had her back to me.

I asked, "You talking to me?"

She answered me with warmth. It was like a conversation between a mother and her child. "Yes, of course I'm talking to you. It's only you and me here."

Her confidence in me was encouraging. But I wondered about the details.

"Sure, why not?" I said. "What do you want me to talk about?"

"Your life," she said.

That was clear enough, but what I'd just agreed to do hadn't fully hit me. Then I asked, somewhat shyly, "Does this pay?"

"Of course," she said. "We pay a lot of people who deliver programs to the State. How much would you charge to be our main speaker?"

I was caught off guard by the idea of getting paid for my speech. And that I would get to decide how much. Getting paid for sharing my thoughts and experiences was both exciting and slightly unreal.

"You mean you're *really* going to pay me?" I asked.

"Yes," she said. "What's your fee?"

"$5,000," I said.

When I realized that I was going to be paid $5,000 to talk about my life, I began to see that my experiences had value and there was power in sharing them. I even invited a young lady to see me speak, a Golden Girl from Mizzou, and I was trying to impress her. I spoke in front of a packed house at a hotel in St. Louis.

Speaking in front of this crowd started a new phase of life for me. It was one of the most exciting and scary things I'd ever done. I started well because I'd memorized the whole speech, but then I messed up halfway through. Someone had walked into the room and I got distracted.

But I stopped, calmed down, and pushed through my feelings to deliver my message. I don't know if anyone heard what I said, but I felt like I connected with everyone there, which only happens when you're being your true self. After everyone stood up and clapped, I sat down and thought about how I'd been brave even though I was scared. Yes, I'd been frightened, but I'd done it anyway, and I was proud of myself. But I still had some doubts, and I quietly looked back over my speech notes under the table.

Mrs. Thomas was kind and encouraging, and that day, I learned two important lessons from her. When the program ended, her face lit up with a big smile and she said, "You were excellent."

I wasn't sure about that and said, "I don't know." Inside my head, I was hard on myself for getting distracted and missing important parts of my speech.

But Mrs. Thomas looked right at me and said, "Orvin, you did great."

Then she gave me my check and that made me feel so much better.

"You asked for what you wanted, told your story, and got a standing ovation," she said with a big, proud smile.

That day, I learned that you have to see your own worth, even if things are hard or broken. I'd never known that the bad things that happened to me could actually be turned into something valuable.

One of the scariest moments of my life was when I told my mother that I'd been sexually abused. But when I stood in front of a room full of people and told them about how I'd been hurt and about all the hard things that had happened to me, it was just as frightening. After my speech, one lady came up to me to say she was glad I was brave enough to share, and that made me cry.

I stayed at the event long after it ended. Many people came and wanted to shake my hand. One person gave me a big hug and whispered, "God loves you."

Another person said, "You're a great example of what we're trying to do in our work."

But the most special moment was when an older lady told me, "We often think we're terribly broken, but even when we're broken, we're still human and complete." She wanted her foster kids to hear my story because she thought it could really help them. I told her about how I like to write as a way to make myself feel better and said she wanted to help her foster kids find their own ways to express themselves through writing or drawing.

Here's what's true: Our stories—your story—can help other people understand their own experiences and figure out where they fit in the world. And, sometimes, when you share these stories, you can earn money too.

She told me, "We don't often get to stop and really see the work we're doing."

That really hit me. She could tell I was afraid, but she thanked me because I made the experience feel real and human to the audience. When I was brave enough to share my story, it changed my life and became an important part of how I connect with the world. I learned that people are naturally drawn to someone who's real and honest, and they want to help. When you're willing to share your true feelings and experiences, you have a special power.

Earning for Myself

About a month before summer ended, I'd saved enough money to pay off my credit card. And then I cut it up into pieces. Yes, you read that right: I destroyed it. I'd also saved enough money to put a down payment on a car, so I bought my first car and signed a lease for my apartment. Other than taking out loans to pay for school, my next big money decisions were paying off that credit card, buying a car, and signing an apartment lease. I'd made these choices by myself, and I felt very proud. I paid my rent for the whole semester instead of monthly, so I wouldn't be tempted to spend money on things I didn't need.

I looked at so many cars to find something I could afford. Most car dealers didn't care that my job was temporary and would end when school started. They only cared that I had a job right then. I thought about whether I could afford the monthly payments during the school year. I also wondered if I would get the extra student loan money like I had the year before. I made myself believe that I'd get it again. If that didn't work out, I would work as many hours as I needed to pay for all my living costs and debts.

I fell in love when I saw my first car, a sky-blue 1987 Buick LeSabre. I put down $1,000 on a car that cost $4,999. I drove the car off the lot with an interest rate that was almost 30 percent. I knew I was moving off campus that year, and since I needed a car, I worked long hours, saved my money, and bought it. By the end of my second year, I'd paid off the car completely. By the end of my third year, I traded it in for a 1999 silver Ford Contour.

During my second year in college, I found my groove. I'd gotten comfortable in my apartment with a very diverse group of roommates: Ben, a white boy from rural Mexico, Missouri; Joey, my Laotian friend from high school; Nate, who was biracial; and me, the Black kid from the inner city. We had great talks about diversity, country versus city life, society, music, food, and life in general. Sometimes we fought about keeping things clean, being too loud, and smoking weed. We also argued about who ate whose food, who played video games all day long, and who had friends over at all hours of the night in our shared living room, which kept everyone awake.

This time in my life was really important. I saw a small version of what America looks like, which included people with different thoughts, appearances, and ways of acting. In our group, everyone later went in a different direction. One roommate joined the military, another got in trouble and went to jail for robbing someone, and another became a dad after falling deeply in love. My path was different from all of theirs and led me to explore where I belonged on campus.

My search for community made me want to learn more about Alpha Phi Alpha, the first historically Black college fraternity in the country. I was looking for diversity, and other than my roommates, the groups I hung out with were often all the same, split by race with very little variety. To connect with Black students, I needed to join Black organizations.

At the same time, I worked almost full-time at JCPenney and got better at customer service and sales skills. That job taught me that success often comes from being able to sell things, whether it's a product, a service, or an idea. But my dream was still to have a career that was about helping others, even though I knew that selling could make more money.

Unfair Treatment

The financial differences between the students at Mizzou were huge, but that didn't change my plans. My goal was clear: to graduate, get a steady job, and live better than my mother had.

I saw that my environment was full of conflict, so I had to be ready for conflict too. I needed to act on the world, but in a different way than I had during childhood. I needed to learn everything I could to prove that I and others who looked like me deserved to be on campus. Many students thought that since Black students had been recruited through Affirmative Action that we didn't deserve to be here. But we weren't there to take things from others that we didn't earn. We were smart and competitive and would make Mizzou and society proud.

At the same time, I believed that a *system failure* had put false barriers around access, opportunities, and success for Black people in the first place. When I talked about the unfair treatment in class discussions, the professor asked, "What is a system?"

My answer stressed the complicated truth about barriers in the system: the laws and rules, both written and unwritten; how society thinks; and behaviors that, even though you can't see them, really affect what's normal, what's expected, and what happens in society. I argued that it was completely unfair for any group to have to prove they deserved to exist, including their right to be part of the campus community.

The more I learned about these issues, the more confident I was in standing up for my right to exist in a society that often felt like it was against me. I became certain that the world isn't fair. I saw that people in power usually don't see anything wrong with keeping things the way they are, while people who don't have power have to prove that they're not defined by their disadvantages.

This personal and community fight against unfair treatment in the system became something I felt deep down, not just an idea connected to the community I came from. Many of my teachers encouraged us to find problems in justice, education, and financial systems and to work with people who wanted to help us reimagine and reshape these systems to make them fair. They said we should get involved in politics to make big, system-wide changes, and they talked about how powerful laws can be.

An important lesson came from Dr. Weems, one of the few Black professors on campus. He stressed that it was important to learn how to work within the system as it exists and find success there. He warned against the trap of negative thoughts, like learned helplessness (which is believing that trying hard won't help you) and victim mentality.

He said, "We aren't victims. Have Black people been hurt by unfair treatment? Yes. But thinking of yourself as a victim means you give up your power."

Even though professors like Dr. Weems created a supportive environment, the campus culture was often unwelcoming. People argued about Affirmative Action, and some classmates said that it was the only reason Black students were at Mizzou. They ignored our talent and ability.

Even if Affirmative Action helped us get in, we still had to keep up our grades, which proved that getting in wasn't enough for success. My academic probation, flunking out, then getting readmitted prove that once we were admitted, we had to meet the university's standards. I strongly believed that fair access to opportunities at public universities should be available for everyone. Then, your success depends on how hard you work, how long you stick with it, and what you achieve.

I told my Black and White friends the same thing I'm telling you: it's your job alone to take hold of an opportunity and make it grow. You can either use it to improve your life or give up when things get hard.

Most of us Black students at Mizzou used that chance to get an education to improve our lives and reach our dreams.

I also wanted to set an example in my classes and in my life. So, I never stopped moving. I worked almost full-time, went to school full-time, studied almost full-time, and didn't have much of a social life like other people did. I was careful to build the right friendships, ones that would help me succeed. I knew I couldn't succeed by myself in this strange new place called college. So, I quickly made friends with professors, and they helped and supported me.

I need to say this again: hard work is necessary, but it isn't enough to achieve success. In college—and in life—you not only have to show up, but you also have to think and work hard. If you do these things, you'll attract the right people into your life who want to help you. A huge part of being successful is having the right people around you.

Right after my best semester ever, I decided to surprise my sister for her graduation. She was the last of us four kids to finish high school. My oldest brother had graduated a while back, and my youngest brother had chosen to go into Job Corps, where he probably got his GED. Last time I checked, he was doing okay living in a small apartment and working at a fast-food restaurant, which seemed like the right choice for him. But I still tried to get him to think about what "more" could look like in his life.

Disaster

In May of 1996, I was driving from Columbia to St. Louis when my cell phone rang. Back then, daytime phone calls cost a lot of money, so I normally didn't answer calls in the morning. I looked at the phone and thought about whether to pick it up. After thinking for a moment I thought, *What the heck?* and answered.

The panicked voice on the other end said, "Orvin, your brother's been shot. Please hurry. We don't know if he'll live. He's at Barnes Hospital."

My brother, Cornelius, was about 18 months younger than me. I was confused and scared, and I pushed my car faster than usual. I knew how serious this was.

I'd felt guilty for leaving Cornelius behind when I went to college, and now the streets might have taken him. As I drove through traffic, my emotions were all over the place. I was crying and angry at the same time. When I got to the hospital, I saw something terrible: my brother was surrounded by machines that were keeping him alive. I had lots of questions and a deep need for answers.

"Will he live?" I asked. The answers weren't clear.

"He can't breathe on his own, and he might be paralyzed," the staff said. I could see how bad his condition was.

"Who did this?" I demanded, trying to understand why this happened and whether the police were trying to catch whoever did it.

Outside his room, I couldn't stop thinking. The few details I had made me want to get revenge. My oldest brother and I, acting on emotion rather than thinking clearly, thought about getting even with whoever had done this.

"We should take care of this ourselves," we decided. We didn't trust the justice system and felt like we had to take action. The need to take control and hurt the people who had hurt my brother was overwhelming. But as the day went on, I realized what this feeling actually was: I felt completely helpless and sad, and that was pushing me toward a path I had no right to take. It became painfully clear that the choices that Cornelius had made are what had set him on a dangerous path.

His friends told me a scary tale of violence that was hard to understand and left me with more questions than answers. Cornelius had been targeted and shot seven or eight times by two different gunmen. There was no doubt in my mind: this was an attempt to take his life, likely rooted in gang conflict. This was overwhelming. I needed a moment to breathe and seek support. So, I stepped outside the hospital to call a friend in Columbia, share the painful news, and seek some comfort.

When I went back, I met Sharon, who said she was the mother of Cornelius's newborn son, Justin.

"What do you mean a son?" I asked, my voice filled with disbelief at this unexpected news.

As I held Justin in my arms for the first time, the weight of our situation truly hit me. Here was a new life tied to the cycle of challenges and hardship that seemed to follow our family. This moment holding my nephew marked a painful realization of the struggles that lay ahead, not just for Cornelius and me, but for this innocent life now caught in the web of our complicated reality.

That week felt darker and darker as I learned that my little sister wouldn't graduate high school. (She would later go on to complete high school and college, and I'm so proud of her!)

When Cornelius came out of his coma, the harsh reality became clear. He was unaware of how serious his situation was, and the doctor delivered news that was nothing short of devastating—he was unlikely to ever move below his neck. This news thrust us into a world of uncertainty and presented a future filled with huge challenges.

My sense of duty toward Cornelius overwhelmed me. Despite our different paths, the bond of brotherhood was unbreakable. Meeting his son, Justin, added another layer to the situation, and the responsibility I felt was even stronger. The thought of coordinating his care and planning for his and Justin's future was scary, but I was determined to find a way forward to be sure that Cornelius got the best possible care, even if it meant re-evaluating my own direction.

This challenging period completely changed my outlook and my life's direction. It strengthened my resolve to finish my education and be accepted into the fraternity, and it pushed me further to eliminate all distractions and focus more intently on my studies. The connections and sense of brotherhood I found through the fraternity became a source of strength that helped me navigate the trials we faced. My recent academic success had already set me on a high, but now I was driven to reach even greater heights, undeterred by the shadows of my past that tried to pull me back. Through it all, I learned to balance my family responsibilities with my personal and academic goals. It was a proof of the resilience and determination my earlier hardships had instilled in me.

TOOLS YOU CAN USE:

New opportunities can show up when you least expect them. What matters is being ready to say "yes" when they do.

1. **Take initiative.** Don't wait for permission to grow. Start where you are.
2. **Be dependable.** When people can count on you, more doors open.
3. **Give back.** Helping others reminds you that you have something valuable to offer the world.

Daily Thought: When you give your best to the world, it has a way of giving back.

Principles 12, 16, and 17 from _The Thriver's Toolkit_ tell you to:

- Work hard and stay dedicated.
- Give back to the community.
- Develop strong leadership skills that inspire others.

CHAPTER 9

NEW AWAKENINGS

"Have a vision. Be demanding."
—*Colin Powell*

"I'm from the bottom, so the top's the only place to go."
—*JAY-Z, "U Don't Know"*

When I went back to Columbia in the summer of 1996, my mind was a whirlwind of concern and determination. I'd pressed the hospital staff for information about Cornelius's immediate future. I understood his paralysis, but I needed to grasp the next steps.

"He needs to learn to breathe on his own," they explained. They said that a stay in a rehabilitation facility would be next.

My initial college goal had been to become a physical therapy major, and despite the competitive nature of the program and the academic setbacks that derailed that dream, I'd learned about the

Rusk Rehabilitation Center, a primary training ground for physical therapy students in Columbia.

"If he can get into that place, it would be great," the hospital staff said.

So that became our goal. Getting Cornelius a spot at Rusk Rehabilitation Center wasn't only about being sure that he received top-notch care; it was also practical for me. Its nearness to campus meant I could be actively involved in his recovery and could support him through this huge change. That summer was defined by responsibility, learning, and pursuing a brighter future for us both.

The path to Cornelius's independence involved several key steps. At first, he had intensive therapy to help him breathe on his own. That was followed by further rehabilitation to strengthen his respiratory system and neck muscles, something that was essential for him to drive a motorized wheelchair. Then, we needed to find a suitable long-term care facility that could meet his needs. The road was challenging and stressful, but having a concrete plan gave me some relief and purpose during this uncertain period.

Professional Opportunities

This period wasn't only about Cornelius's recovery. It was also a pivotal stage in my personal and professional development. In addition to returning to campus, I had an opportunity to be part of the management internship program at JCPenney. Encouraged by Dan, the men's department manager, I considered this new opportunity. Dan had seen potential in me and recommended me for the program.

We often chatted during my shifts. Once, he asked me, "So, what's your major again?"

"Social work," I said. "I'm thinking about going to grad school but am feeling my way through the core classes."

Dan saw a different potential in me. "You're a hard worker, got plenty of drive. Ever thought about a career in retail? You don't need a Master of Social Work; you could get a graduate degree in JCPenney. You could really go places here," he said.

He caught me off guard. While I like my work at Penney's, I'd never thought about retail as a career. My passion was to help others, and I didn't see a connection between retail work and helping others. *And what's a graduate degree in JCPenney?* I wondered.

Dan was joking with that comment, but his point was that if I applied myself, I'd advance my career. His talks about the opportunities in retail, and that you could make a lot of money by climbing the ranks from store to district manager, sparked a new curiosity in me.

"Store managers do quite well for themselves," he said, "and district managers even more so." Knowing that I'd been a foster kid, he added, "This would also let you help your family."

My thoughts raced with the possibilities. I'd told my younger siblings that I would prove that we could succeed. So, I explored the program he suggested and found out that it covered many aspects, from merchandising to finance. The idea of a well-paying career in retail began to appeal to me.

"What's the catch?" I finally asked, half-joking.

Dan was honest about the sacrifices, particularly the long hours during holidays and major sporting events.

"Yes, there are trade-offs," he admitted, "but those are also the times when we rake in the most revenue. It's all part of being successful in retail. We have to be open when our customers want to shop."

The lessons I learned and my success in that internship opened up a new realm of professional opportunities. The insights I'd gained had enriched my point of view and equipped me with valuable skills and experiences that would shape my future choices. I reminded myself that the journey ahead was filled with potential and promise, ready to be seized.

When autumn came, my relationship with my family, especially Cornelius, evolved as I navigated these shifting dynamics. Despite his struggle with his new life at Rusk Rehabilitation Center, I encouraged him to look beyond his physical limitations and not view himself as a victim.

I introduced him to Tyrone Flowers, a paraplegic law student and future fraternity brother who had a life of purpose and optimism despite his challenges. Tyrone had also been shot multiple times by a basketball teammate, but he didn't let that derail him. Not only did he graduate, he was now enrolled in law school and married to a smart and attractive woman. He was deeply rooted in his Christian faith and was focused on helping others overcome their challenges. He was living a full life, and that's what I wanted Cornelius to see.

I hoped Cornelius would be inspired by Tyrone like I was, but none of my encouragement or connections with inspiring people moved him. There was no reaching Cornelius. After he could breathe on his own, I got a call that he was checking himself out of the rehab center and moving to another place far away in Illinois. Cornelius's decision to move away marked a significant turn. He'd chosen a path that was different from the support network we'd hoped to provide. Even though I didn't like his decision, I had to respect his independence.

Cornelius's decision and some other family turmoil kept pulling me back and made me wonder, *Can I achieve success if I don't eliminate the distractions of family life?*

I remembered something about airplanes: "Put your mask on first." I didn't have my mask on.

Broken Relationships

I was fragile, and any support I hoped to get from Joyce was shattered when my caseworker called to check in on me.

"How are you?" she asked

"I'm fine," I answered.

"Do you need anything?"

"No, except for money. I work every day, but it's tough," I said.

"Are you still receiving the two-hundred-dollar monthly maintenance check?" she asked.

"No," I admitted. "I thought it stopped when I came to college."

"No, they didn't stop," she clarified. "Let me verify the address where the checks are being sent."

Apparently, the checks had been sent to my previous address—and were cashed by Joyce.

My stomach dropped as I sat on the edge of the bed, staring at the floor. The late-afternoon light flickered through the blinds, and for a moment, I couldn't tell if it was anger or sadness burning in my chest.

"Are you sure?" I asked.

"Yes, I am," she affirmed. "I need to report this."

I asked her not to report the missing checks, and she agreed.

When I later talked to Joyce, she wasn't sorry. She said it was fair payment for letting me stay in her home during my senior year. That conversation ended our relationship and tested my resolve. But it didn't erase my love or gratitude for Joyce and her family. They had been kind to me, and I would always appreciate that.

Losing Joyce as a confidant hurt. I had considered her family, and I believed she'd chosen me too. But I was mistaken. Our connection, I realized, was more functional than familial. It had been built on mutual exchange, not deep belonging.

Joyce was always kind, and I cared deeply for her. But I was wounded, and when I'm wounded, I withdraw. That was how I coped. I only spoke to her once more on the day I introduced her to the woman who would become my wife.

Despite my love for my brother and sister, the years before and during college had widened the distance between us. Our family bonds were breaking. It didn't mean we stopped caring or trying to support each other, but our times together were rare. When we did connect, our conversations often circled back to our difficult childhood.

At the same time, I pulled away from others too. It was my way of protecting myself. Most of my interactions had a purpose; I talked to people only when necessary. Trusting anyone else felt hard. This wasn't new for me, but it was stronger now, and it shaped all my relationships.

Since I wasn't close to my family, I tried to build a group of friends who could be like a "quasi-family." But even those relationships had to benefit both sides. When they didn't, I backed away.

Most of us think family relationships are the most important ones but sometimes they're not. I learned that lesson in one of my early projects in the School of Social Work. My assignment was to interview someone who was openly gay.

I set up the meeting and stood outside his apartment, pacing and practicing my questions. My heart raced. It was the first time I'd ever been alone with a gay man.

When he opened the door, his big personality filled the space. "Welcome, Orvin," he said with a smile. "I'm excited we're going to do this."

As we sat in his small living room, I suddenly felt the walls closing in, forcing us closer. What's the deal? I thought. Why am I feeling this way? Then I remembered what one of my professors had said: "Every gay man you meet isn't interested in you." I laughed silently and relaxed.

Dominic told me about his coming-out experience. It was painful. His relationship with his parents was strained, and they rarely spoke. That forced him to build his own circle of support.

"That's what it's like for most of us," he said, bowing his head. "People, including family, can be incredibly cruel. We're real humans too."

We talked for hours. I told him I understood his pain. I, too, felt like an outsider—disconnected from childhood friends and distant from my family. By the time our conversation ended, my ideas about inclusion and diversity had expanded. I had a new level of empathy for people whose stories were different from mine.

Dominic's experience, and my own, cemented my belief that family isn't defined only by blood. True family is made up of people who choose to bond, support one another, and share values, memories, and experiences.

These relationships work when both sides give and receive, when there's genuine connection. Some bonds last a lifetime; others don't. Joyce was indeed family to me—just not forever.

Building a family from friendships gave me a new way to think about what it means to create and sustain meaningful relationships in life.

Spiritual Awakening

I started to question everything. I wondered why God had spared me, and I thought back to my teenage years when I marched with the Nation of Islam to reclaim my North St. Louis city neighborhood. I wondered whether the Islam faith fit better with my place in life and if it was relevant to me as a Black man. The mostly White depictions of Christ didn't look anything like me, and I wondered why.

I started dating people from different backgrounds. This challenged what I believed and led me to explore new spiritual ideas.

When I dated different people, I visited their churches and began a spiritual journey. I started questioning the beliefs I'd had since I was a kid.

I talked to very religious people about all the different types of Christian churches. This complicated my spiritual understanding. I learned to think about Christianity like school subjects. Christianity was the major, and different types like Baptist, Methodist, and others were like minors.

Now I had a way to understand the different kinds of faith much better.

I realized that my attraction to the Nation of Islam was because they were the loudest group that offered an alternative to mainstream perceptions. They valued Black traits that others often thought were bad. They said you had to love yourself before you could love others. They wanted Black people to rely on themselves and build their own power. Their teachings about accepting your own worth and rejecting what society forced on you really spoke to me. They pushed me to create my own path and earn respect by being self-sufficient.

And I had a significant awakening. While sitting in Tyrone's apartment, I wholeheartedly welcomed Christ into my life as a young adult. I'd been baptized years earlier in my Catholic church, but this was different. I wasn't saying this because someone told me it was the right thing to do or because I wanted to please the adults in my life. This was my choice. My focus was on the essential teachings of Christ and the Bible alone, and I was reborn and set free from what other people expected of me. College made me realize that my Christian faith had to deal with real problems happening right now.

I found a Christian community that cared about people and worked to fight unfair treatment in society. The churches that connected with me mixed Black liberation ideas with smart thinking and matched what I really believed in.

The artwork in my apartment showed Christ as a Black man and a Black father holding his son. These pictures meant my faith was coming back. They reminded me that I could see Christ in myself.

My new faith gave me an anchor and kept me steady when life got unpredictable. It supported me as I moved through a world that often questioned my worth. Sometimes the world saw me as important, and sometimes it ignored me. But my faith opened doors to forgiveness, deeper relationships, and it healed old hurts from the past. It's surprising how much you can change and heal when you commit to your spiritual life again.

Faith became my guiding light. It took away my fear and showed me a path of forgiveness and hope. It became more than just comfort. It shaped my work values, which replaced criticism and hate with compassion and understanding. My spiritual journey became a crucial part of my story. It gave me wisdom about my decisions and goals and a strong belief.

My new commitment to Christianity went hand-in-hand with my love for social work. It helped me understand other people and made me determined to rise above my past. This combination made me believe even more in unconditional love and kindness. I argued for treating everyone with dignity and respect, no matter what they looked like, where they came from, how much money they had, or what they'd done. These ideas came straight from my faith, and it gave me a voice to use my own story and what I'd learned to fight for social change.

Fraternity Life

The fall semester wasn't just about my classes, it was also a time to build deeper connections through the fraternity.

Fraternities and sororities on college campuses represent brotherhood and sisterhood—people you choose to be in relationship with, different from the family you're born into. This was my first real attempt to reframe my network and surround myself with people who cared about me and shared similar goals—graduating from college and starting meaningful careers.

Planning parties and events helped strengthen those friendships. It mixed fun with purpose and built connections that lasted beyond campus life.

For me, Alpha Phi Alpha Fraternity represented the ideals I wanted to live by. Luminaries like Dr. Martin Luther King Jr., Thurgood Marshall, and Duke Ellington (all Alpha men) weren't just names in history books. They were examples of excellence, leadership, and impact.

During my interview with Dominic, the openly gay student who also struggled with family connections, he said something I never forgot: "It's easier to operate in the world when you don't have to pretend to be something you're not."

He was right. Joining the fraternity would test my determination to stay true to myself. It would challenge me to belong without losing my identity. When they asked why I wanted to join, I told them it was because of the history and values of the men who had worn those letters before me and because I needed that brotherhood.

On the night I received my letters, I stood shoulder to shoulder with my new brothers in Rothwell Gym. Though at a party, the campus was quiet, and the stars looked close enough to touch. I ran my hand over the stitched letters on my jacket and thought, *This is who I've become.*

My life became a balance of school, personal growth, and social responsibility. Alpha Phi Alpha's values of scholarship, manly deeds, and love for all mankind pushed me to stay focused and finish strong, even with the distractions of college life.

My path to joining the fraternity was more than a desire to belong. It was a promise to live by the values of excellence, leadership, and service. I didn't have a backup plan, and every choice mattered. I stayed focused on my goals because I believed my future was mine to create through faith, hard work, and a clear vision of who I wanted to become.

Fraternity life was even better than I expected. It gave me brotherhood, and through our connection with the women of Alpha Kappa Alpha Sorority, sisterhood too. But there was something I hadn't realized at first: Black Greeks received the same kind of attention on campus that athletes did. That visibility made social life easier and opened doors to leadership roles in both the School of Social Work and the fraternity.

Still, I was careful with my time. I chose my moments to get involved and didn't give in to peer pressure. I stayed true to my commitment to be my authentic self even when that drew criticism. But I found my rhythm.

Outside the fraternity, I wrote poetry, spoke at events across Missouri, and shared my story. Those experiences taught me that leadership isn't about fitting in, it's about standing firm in who you are.

Crossroads

As graduation approached, I reached another crossroads. I started thinking seriously about my next move. I'd been offered a job at JC Penney for $30,000 a year, but I argued that it was less than my $31,000 in student loan debt. They eventually matched my number, but even with the raise, I couldn't shake the feeling that retail wasn't my calling.

So, I made a different choice. I decided to pursue a Master of Social Work. I wanted to do work that mattered, work that helped people. I believed that if I followed my purpose, the money would come later. That decision led me to Integration Plus (Planned Living with University Support), a program run by the Department of Mental Health for kids with dual diagnoses.

At first, the work was tough. One of my first cases involved a boy who often mumbled, "Kill mom, dad." His speech was slurred, his emotions unpredictable, and his obsession with tornadoes made him spin toys or himself in violent circles. It was challenging, but it also reminded me of the trauma, confusion, and chaos I'd once lived through in places like the Annie Malone Children's Home. Despite the difficulty, I found deep meaning in the work. Helping those kids wasn't just a job, it was part of my healing.

Meeting Her

I didn't know it at the time, but my life was about to take a big turn after I attended a Mike Tyson pay-per-view fight at a fraternity brother's duplex. I arrived early to make sure I had a place to sit because everyone wanted to see Iron Mike fight in the mid-1990s. The first floor was packed. In addition to the fight, I had a romantic interest in one of the young ladies I knew would be attending the event. She was a part of the sorority Delta Sigma Theta, founded in 1913, as one of the original Black Greek letter organizations.

As the night went on, I saw a different woman sitting on the arm of the loveseat just a few feet from me. I'd find out later she was in the same sorority. She had brown skin and wore a faux leather jacket with nice-fitting pants. Her hair looked perfect, and her hazel eyes really stood out. She was short, about five feet tall, with a fit body that her clothes showed off well.

We started talking in a playful, teasing way. I joked with her about her "real hair and real eyes" and made fun of her faux leather jacket. She laughed at my jokes and wasn't upset. Nothing major happened that night between us, but Tyson's quick win in the boxing match was definitely the best part of the evening.

The night ended and I said goodbye to everyone. I looked one last time at "Faux Jacket" and hoped for a sign that something might happen between us. But nothing did. We went our separate ways, and I wondered about what could've been. Since nothing happened, I kept dating other girls and eventually became semi-exclusive with a different girl who was fun to be around and was really nice. We spent a lot of time together, and as I got closer to graduation, I started to think about having a relationship that would last beyond college. Even though I usually kept people at a distance, I became more open to building something closer and more serious.

I finished well and completed my undergraduate degree successfully. But this milestone, even though it was important, felt kind of empty because it no longer matched how high I wanted to reach. I wanted to pursue excellence as far as I could go.

On my birthday in December 1998, I reached a goal that had once seemed impossible: I got my Bachelor of Social Work degree. Since I'd cut my course load to twelve hours, this took an extra semester. So, the moment was kind of anticlimactic, both emotionally and practically. I was already focused on beating the next challenge: finishing the graduate program at Mizzou in only a year and a half to make up for lost time.

Latriece

It had been months since the new calendar year began, and I hadn't given much thought to the encounter with the mystery woman, "Faux Jacket," whom I'd met at the party. But one day we reconnected. I remembered her face and the context of our conversation at the Tyson fight months ago, but I didn't remember her name—bad form.

We struck up a conversation, and I teased, "Why are you in my building?"

She said she was taking an organizational theory class as an elective, and this just happened to be where it was offered. I couldn't find any words to keep the conversation going, and I was clearly attracted to this woman, so I enthusiastically said, "I get a hard-on for organizational theory."

She froze and looked shocked. "What?"

I explained further. "I love social work and the theory that supports it, particularly how organizational systems impact people." As we were about to part ways, I gathered the courage to ask for her phone number.

She hesitated and questioned, "Orvin, do you even remember my name?"

I winced at the truth and was shocked that she remembered mine. "We both know the answer to that," I replied softly.

I admitted that I didn't recall her name and made a futile effort to remember it before she said, "Do your research."

I jokingly asked her not to hold it against me. Eventually, I gave her my number and asked skeptically, "Are you going to call me?" I repeated the question like an insecure teenager several times as we went our separate ways, focused in her direction as I walked backwards, trying not to trip while I made my last plea, "Will you call me?"

She called that night. Actually, her first question was, "What's my name?"

"Latriece is your name," I thundered with the confidence of someone who was connected and could find things out. Before I had even gotten back to my apartment, I called around to my fraternity brothers and found out that her name was Latriece.

One of them later said, "She's out of your league."

Maybe she was, but I almost immediately felt that this was different. We talked until very late at night with quiet breaks, which meant that one of us had fallen asleep. I learned that she was a business major, accounting to be exact. She was at the end of a five-year program where she would graduate with a master's degree in accountancy. She was an only child, and both her mom and dad were still in her life, though she had a strained and complicated relationship with her dad. She had a big family and loved her grandma, and since her early teen years, she'd been in a couple of long-term relationships.

After that, I spent every waking moment with Latriece, and every moment when I wasn't with her, I thought about her. Latriece was serious-minded. She wanted something out of life. She was going to succeed because she was disciplined. This intensified my attraction. This was what I needed in my life—someone who had a sense of purpose and a strong work ethic and who could make it without me—because I still believed my life would end early.

One day during those early weeks, we went to Walmart to buy a few items. While we stood in the checkout line, she unexpectedly added a candy bar.

I jokingly protested, "I'm not paying for that candy."

She replied, "Quit playing."

I said more firmly, "I'm not paying for this candy bar."

What started as a joke quickly spiraled out of control, and I got frustrated with the swift shift from her request to making a demand. In my mind, I was not going to be pushed around. I thought, *I'm not a defenseless kid. I need to stand my ground!*

She then suggested, "Fine, give me the keys to the car, so I can get my wallet."

I refused.

By now, the checkout cashier's face was flushed, clearly flustered by the charged atmosphere between us. It didn't take long to realize my mistake and take responsibility for what was happening. We went back to the car, and Latriece asked me to take her home.

That night, we didn't speak. But I soon learned that Latriece had reacted to what seemed like my controlling demeanor. I was at fault for initiating the conflict, but I had reacted to what I saw as her demanding attitude. This pattern repeated itself multiple times in our relationship.

I had already playfully asked her to marry me on multiple occasions, drawn to her strength. However, something about that Walmart incident made me pause. I didn't know if we were the right personality fit. We were two strong-willed individuals who had just recently met. I wondered, *what are the chances that we can overcome the odds and lead a successful life?*

Despite our differences, we worked through that fight. After the thirteenth time of playfully proposing and her saying yes, I decided I should get her a ring. I went to a mall in Columbia, opened a line of credit with Kay Jeweler, and bought her a ring. I spent $5,000 on that ring! It was a nice diamond with a gold band, less than one carat, and it was perfect.

Latriece always wondered why I'd asked her to marry me so many times and why I didn't have the courage to make one real proposal. There were several reasons, but mostly, being emotionally vulnerable was challenging for me. I displayed all the symptoms of someone who'd endured a traumatic life. Managing my emotions, memories, and anxiety from years of abuse was hard. Negative thoughts were my constant companions, and I worked hard to cope with them. I often dealt with mild depression, felt numb, disconnected, and unable to trust, and I usually pushed people away before they became too intimate.

Latriece and I were polar opposites when it came to romantic relationships. She was capable of deep love, whereas I wrestled with it. In a display of youthful naivety, I often said at the start of any relationship, "This won't last," thus making it inevitable.

After four weeks of dating Latriece, my fears seemed to come true, and they shook the foundation of my trust. I discovered that she'd ended a long-term relationship with her high school sweetheart just a day before we met, a relationship that had continued on and off throughout college. I was heartbroken because I felt like I'd been deceived. If I'd known this at the beginning, I wouldn't have pursued Latriece because my insecurities, fear of abandonment, and my unwillingness to open up were huge problems.

But instead of retreating, I came to an unusual solution. I decided the next logical step was not to continue dating but to speed things up, to move in together and get married, despite only having known her for a short time. This plan, oddly enough, seemed perfectly reasonable to me at the time and was driven by a deep desire for real companionship.

Then, one summer day, on my thirteenth proposal, Latriece finally gave in with a playful, "Boy, I said yes, I would marry you."

That's when I showed her the ring and made our commitment real. She was surprised that my playful questions had turned into a ring. I don't think either of us had expected this gesture of commitment so soon. I didn't know exactly what I was doing, but I felt like I needed to do it. It was another one of those "do it scared" moments.

"Of all the girls, why me?" Latriece once asked. It was obvious to me: we had a connection I didn't have with anyone else. She was stubborn when she set her mind to something and appreciated my kindness. After about two weeks into our relationship, I paid off her $5,000 credit card bill. I did it because I cared for her and didn't want her to struggle to pay the card. I also paid the bill as a test. She didn't pull away; in fact, she didn't move one way or another. She stayed right where she was—close.

She appreciated my spirit and drive, and never once questioned whether I would do what I said I would do. She showed care and concern for her friends. She didn't drink much, and she didn't run the streets. She was thoughtful and often cooked or just hung out with me wherever I wanted to be. She loved God. She knew what she wanted out of a relationship. She was thoughtful about her mother, father, and grandmother. She showed depth in her emotions and thoughts. She was attractive. She was the best of every girl I had ever dated and more. She was real. What you saw was what you got. She was a perfect 10 for me, and she was definitely out of my league!

We had met at a really important time in her career. She was finishing up her graduate program and taking tests for her CPA license—something she needed to start a successful career as an accountant. While we were dating, she got distracted from school and didn't do as well on her CPA exam as she could have. But her grades were excellent, and she'd gotten an audit job with one of the top accounting firms in St. Louis. She'd also found an apartment and set her move-in date.

When I gave her the ring, I asked her to move in with me instead of going to St. Louis. I wanted her to delay the move and marry me as soon as possible. I'd never felt love like this before. I was scared I'd lose her if she moved back to St. Louis without me, and I wasn't willing to take that chance.

So, we got married within three months of our unlikely meeting in front of that concrete social work building. She was 22, and I was the older man at 24. On a sunny day, June 4, 1999, we both took lunch breaks from our jobs in Jefferson City. She worked for Claire McCaskill, who was the State Auditor then, and I was an intern at the Missouri Association of Social Welfare, a group that fought for equality and social justice in Missouri.

I don't remember much about the ceremony. The judge asked if we were there because we wanted to be, and we both said yes. We signed some papers, left the courthouse, had lunch, and went back to work. I never told anyone on campus. Latriece hadn't told her mother yet, and we didn't want people judging us by saying, "But you've only known each other for three months. What a challenge!"

We lived in our college town for a few months and took time to write down a vision for our family, one that would be completely different from what our parents had experienced. We talked about commitment, faith, staying together no matter what, raising children, owning a home, building businesses, and growing our careers.

Before moving to St. Louis for her new job, we made a promise to never give up on what we wanted to achieve personally and professionally. For the next year, I drove back and forth between St. Louis and Columbia while working at Integration Plus and finishing my first graduate degree, a Master of Social Work.

Within the first three months, we finally told her mother. But we kept our marriage a secret from everyone else, including her large, curious family. Her mom was crushed to have missed this important day in her daughter's life because Latriece was her only child. We'd always planned to have a proper church ceremony, so we decided to have a church wedding one year later at Mount Beulah Missionary Baptist Church in St. Louis. It was a happy but complicated time in our young relationship, but it marked a beginning—our beginning.

Tools You Can Use:

Awakening is what happens when you realize your life has meaning—even the painful parts. It's when you start seeing yourself not as a survivor, but as a Thriver.

1. **Dream with direction.** It's one thing to imagine a better life; it's another to plan how to make it real.
2. **Be bold enough to be yourself.** The world doesn't need copies—it needs your authentic voice.
3. **Keep growing.** Every time you learn something new, you open a new door for your future self.

Daily Thought: The more you grow into who you really are, the clearer your purpose becomes.

Principles 8, 19, and 20 from *The Thriver's Toolkit* tell you to:

- Embrace lifelong learning as a way of growing stronger.
- Believe your future is positive and filled with purpose.
- Be vulnerable and authentic—it's how real growth begins.

EPILOGUE

Sometimes I still wake up early, like I did as a kid—
the same boy who once lay awake in fear,
now waking in peace.
The difference is, today I wake up thankful.
Most mornings, before the sun rises, I walk through the quiet of
my house and whisper,
"Thank you, God,"
the same way I once whispered,
"Please help me,"
as a child trying to fall asleep.

People often ask me,
"How did you make it?"
When I hear that, I think about how far God has brought me.
I think about how, through faith, hard work, and the support of others,
I've lived a life fuller than I ever imagined.
Less than three percent of kids who age out of foster care finish college,
and I could have been one of the many who didn't.
But I did— and I've done much more since.
Now, don't misinterpret that.
For you, "college" might mean a trade school, a two-year degree, or a four-year degree—
or maybe something entirely different.
The point isn't the type of school or the title you chase.
The point is that I decided to do something more with my life when the chances that I would were slim.
And that choice—to keep learning, to keep reaching—changed everything.
You have options.
You have the right to think for yourself and to follow the path that fits the purpose God placed in you.
Don't let the world box you in or convince you that there's only one way to succeed.
You don't have to bend to what the world suggests you should do or be.
Let faith guide your choices, and let your choices reflect your faith.
Following your passion is important—but so is understanding your purpose.
Passion gives you energy, but purpose gives that energy direction.
When you do what you love and use it to help others, success follows in its own time.

Don't chase money; chase meaning.
If you stay faithful to your purpose, the resources will come.
I've learned that when your heart is in the right place, God can use your gifts anywhere—
in a classroom, on a construction site, behind a counter, or in a corner office.

People have said, "You're entitled not to be okay after all you've faced."
But I am okay.
In fact, I'm thriving.

My life has taken me through many careers,
but the mission has always been the same—helping people.
Whether leading nonprofits, building communities, or running a bank,
I've learned that every kind of work can be God's work
when done with integrity and love.

Professionally, I've done well—and yes, financially too.
That matters because it means I can create opportunities for others,
give back, and invest in the people and places that raised me.
I believe we need more people of faith,
especially people who come from the most challenged backgrounds,
to build wealth with integrity—
because wealthy people can fund the Kingdom of God
and bring resources where they're needed most.

God has blessed me in ways that go far beyond anything I could've imagined as a kid born in East St. Louis, Illinois and raised in North City, St. Louis, Missouri.
I don't worry about bills anymore—I have more than enough to make ends meet,
to save for the future,
and to help others.

Sometimes I catch myself standing in the wide hallway of my house,
remembering how, as a kid, I could take three steps and be in every room of our shotgun apartment.
Now I live in a home with thousands of square feet, an indoor pool, and a workout room—
a far cry from where I started.
I can afford to drive any car I want, but that's not what I value most.
True wealth isn't about what you park in the driveway—
it's about what you build inside your heart and home.

Money gives you options, but faith gives you peace.
And when you use your success to lift others,
you find something even greater than wealth—you find purpose.

I travel the world for work and for joy—Paris, London, Cuba, Iceland, Portugal, the continent of Africa, and more.
I've stood on balconies overlooking cities I once only saw in magazines,
but I still remember the cracked sidewalk outside our apartment on Wabada Ave.
Those contrasts remind me that grace carried me from fear to freedom.

When I was younger, like you, I used to think dreaming was enough—
until the day I was with older people who seemed to dream a lot but never achieved anything significant
and realized they didn't do the work.
That day I learned: faith without focus doesn't build anything.

When my kids were little, they would chase each other through the house, and
their laughter bounced off the walls while my wife was trying to bring order to their chaos. This was something I once could only imagine.
In that moment, I felt God's redemption in real time.

Because real success isn't just about getting ahead;
it's about finding peace where you are.
But the best part of my story isn't the money or the titles.
It's the peace that comes from healing,
the strength that comes from faith,
and the love that comes from family.
I'm emotionally stronger, mentally healthier, and spiritually grounded
in ways I never dreamed possible.
I have a family that loves me through my challenges—
proof that love really can rewrite a life.
When I look back at the kid I used to be—
scared, uncertain, and just trying to survive—
I realize that my whole life has been a demonstration project.
A demonstration project shows what's possible
when an idea comes to life.
That's what I hope my life does for you.
I learned that every dream needs discipline.
Every goal needs a plan.
Every plan needs prayer.
And every prayer needs faith that doesn't quit.
When the world says, "Wait your turn,"
faith says, "Walk in purpose."
I'm grateful—not just for what I've gained,
but for who I've become.
Everything I once thought disqualified me,
God used to qualify me.
My pain had a purpose.
My story became a seed.
And now, it's your turn.
To build.
To believe.

To give.
To grow.
So as you finish this book, remember:
You can rise.
You can build.
You can heal.
You can lead.
You can become more than a conqueror.
Because if I made it—through faith, focus, and hard work—
you can too.

A Final Word to You

You are not your pain.
You are not your past.
You are a work in progress—and that's powerful.
You were created for something greater than struggle.
Don't let fear, comparison, or doubt convince you otherwise.
To keep growing, you'll need to do three things that
changed my life:
Reframe your thinking—start seeing problems as
possibilities.
Reclaim your agency—remember that your choices shape your
future.
Rename your network—surround yourself with people who build,
not break, your belief.
You have what it takes to change your story,
to build wealth and wisdom,
and to live a life that lifts others.
Whatever your dream is,
give it your best,
trust God with the rest,
and never forget—
you are already becoming more than a conqueror.

And One Last Thing

The boy who once felt invisible now lives fully seen—
by God, by others, and by himself.

When I stand on a stage and look out at a crowd of
accomplished leaders,
or receive invitations to speak to young people,
I sometimes picture that little boy sitting in the back of
the room—
and smile, because now he knows he belongs.

I'm still learning, still growing, still becoming—
but every day, I thank God that I didn't give up.

Without faith, I would've stopped believing that my story
could change—
and when you stop believing, you stop building.

So start where you are,
use what you have,
and trust that faith will carry you
where fear never could.

And as you rise, remember—
when you lift others, you multiply the miracle.

That's how we change the world—
one believer,
one builder,
one conqueror at a time.

Tools You Can Use: Faith, Purpose, and Money

Gratitude Focus:

Be thankful for what you have right now, even if it doesn't feel like
much. Gratitude opens your eyes to see how far you've already
come and helps you make wise choices with what's in your hands
today.

Reflection / Why It Matters:
Money is a tool, not the goal. When you use it with purpose, it can change your life and bless others too. Faith gives you the courage to dream big, and purpose helps you aim those dreams in the right direction. If you chase money, you'll always need more. But if you chase meaning, you'll always have enough.

Scripture:

"For where your treasure is, there your heart will be also."
—Matthew 6:21

Lesson:

1. **Faith first.** Believe that God has given you gifts that can create value—that's the real foundation of wealth.
2. **Purpose next.** Ask yourself, "How can what I'm good at help others?" Purpose turns talent into impact.
3. **Money last.** Learn how to earn it, save it, invest it, and give it—but never let it define you.

Your Turn:

- What's one thing you're passionate about that could grow into a purpose?
- Who do you admire for how they handle success or money, and why?
- What's one small financial habit you can start now—saving, budgeting, giving—that reflects your faith and future goals?

Challenge:
Reframe your thinking about money—see it as a resource, not a reason.
Reclaim your agency—take ownership of your financial future.
Rename your network—surround yourself with people who inspire you to grow and give.

Your faith will lead you to purpose.
Your purpose will attract opportunities.
And your discipline will build a life that's both prosperous and peaceful.

ACKNOWLEDGMENTS

I want to thank every person who ever mentored me, coached me, taught me, sponsored me, or simply believed in me when I couldn't yet believe in myself. You showed me what it means to be seen, guided, and loved in moments when I didn't even know I needed it.

To every mentor who took time to teach me something new, thank you for showing me that growth is a lifelong process. To every teacher who challenged me to think bigger, thank you for planting seeds of curiosity and confidence. To every coach who pushed me to give more when I wanted to quit, thank you for teaching me discipline and heart.

To every sponsor and supporter who opened a door or gave me a chance—you reminded me that opportunity and faith walk hand in hand. You proved that a little encouragement can change the direction of someone's life.

To the people who work every day in schools, youth programs, foster care, community centers, and churches—thank you for investing in young people. You are shaping the next generation of leaders, dreamers, and conquerors. The hours you give, the patience you show, and the love you extend are building futures you may never see but are changing lives all the same.

To my friends and "day ones," who have stood with me through every stage of life—thank you for keeping me grounded. Real friends remind you of where you came from while cheering for where you're going.

To my family, who have loved me through every high and low—thank you for reminding me that love doesn't have to be perfect to be powerful.

And to my wife and children—thank you for your patience, laughter, and faith in me. You remind me daily that purpose begins at home.

Finally, to every person reading this who has chosen to *pour into someone else*—a child, a student, a neighbor, a friend—thank you. You are proof that one act of care can ripple across generations.

This book is not just about my journey; it's about *our journey*— the power of what happens when people lift one another up. If you've ever helped someone see what's possible, you are part of this story too.

ABOUT THE AUTHOR

When he was a kid, Orvin "Orv" Kimbrough thought he might grow up to be Superman. He didn't end up wearing a cape, but his imagination—just like yours can—took him further than he ever dreamed.

Orv grew up in East St. Louis, Illinois, where life was hard. His mom did her best to raise him and his brothers and sister, but their neighborhood was filled with poverty and pain. When Orv was only eight years old, his mother passed away, and he and his siblings entered the foster care system. That's where his journey to becoming more than a conqueror began.

He lived in different children's homes and learned early that sometimes life is unfair—but it can also build your strength if you don't give up. He discovered that education, hard work, and faith could open doors that once felt locked.

Over time, Orv earned college and graduate degrees and learned that how you learn is just as important as what you learn. He also discovered that every kind of work—whether in a classroom, a company, or a community—can be God's work when it's done with purpose and love.

Before he ever worked in banking, Orv spent twenty years helping people through nonprofits, including leading one of the largest

United Way organizations in the country. Today, as author of the award-winning *Twice over a Man* and *Ward and the State*, he serves as the Chairman and CEO of Midwest BankCentre, helping families buy homes, small businesses grow, and communities thrive.

But Orv doesn't measure success by titles or money. He measures it by impact, by how many people he can help see what's possible for their own lives.

He believes in three simple but powerful ideas:

- Reframe your thinking.
- Reclaim your power.
- Rename your circle.

Because how you think, how you act, and who you surround yourself with can change everything.

Orv still dreams big, but now his dream is to help you dream big too—to help you see that your imagination can take you farther than fear ever will.

His life is proof that your past doesn't define your future, your choices do. He hopes this book helps you believe that, no matter what you've been through, you can rise, rebuild, and become more than a conqueror.

For more information or to connect with Orv,
visit orvinkimbrough.com.

www.ingramcontent.com/pod-product-compliance
Lightning Source LLC
Chambersburg PA
CBHW071748120626
46550CB00002B/712